NOT JUST SOMEBODY'S DAUGHTER

A BIBLICAL STUDY ON RESTORATION FROM THE DAMAGE OF SEXUAL ABUSE

NOT JUST SOMEBODY'S DAUGHTER

A BIBLICAL STUDY ON **RESTORATION** FROM THE DAMAGE OF SEXUAL ABUSE

SARAH JANE HO

Not Just Somebody's Daughter: A Biblical Study on Restoration from the Damage of Sexual Abuse

2015 © by Sarah Jane Ho

Indie Publishing & Design Services by

Melinda Martin | TheHelpyHelper.com

ISBN-13: 978-0692448922 (notyetproverbs31)

ISBN-10: 0692448926

ACKNOWLEDGEMENTS

I want to say thank you to my Beta Readers:

Mom, thank you for your support and confidence in me,
Jamie for speaking truth in love,
Rebecca for your constant encouragement,
Curtis for your unbiased wisdom,
and Bethany for going above and beyond the call of duty.

I also want to thank Alicia for her mentorship filled with a
wealth of knowledge, for suggesting that this book become a study
guide, her proof-reading skills, and the constant dedication in
helping me achieve my goals.

Last, my editor, Melinda, for anticipating my every move with
the most effective answers and creating a stunning
display of my heart.

DEDICATION

This book is dedicated to the dads in my life.

To Raymond, the daddy who raised me,
thank you for letting me be your pride and joy, loving me despite
my multitude of flaws, and I will see you again in Heaven wor-
shipping in awe at His feet.

To Paul, the man who married my mom when she lost my dad,
thank you for effortlessly picking up where he left off.

Finally, to the love of my life, my husband David, thank you,
lovebug, for being the head of our household, spiritual leader,
and parenting beside me as we protect the purity of our children
(Summer, Faith, Abigail, Hadassah, and Levi) who daily display a
beautiful innocence that we are proud to nurture.

TESTIMONIALS

"I just finished reading *Not Just Somebody's Daughter: A Biblical Study on Restoration from Sexual Abuse*. It is a powerful story of deep-seated struggles with identity after abuse and triumph over the sin that followed. I found myself up late into the night as I read through similar struggles I had faced. The Lord led me to *Not Just Somebody's Daughter* so that I could find the answers I have been struggling with since childhood."

Jenn Gerlach, SimpleAtHome.com

"*Not Just Somebody's Daughter: A Biblical Study on Restoration from Sexual Abuse* is simply written and will be well-received by other teens/women who have found themselves in similar circumstances. Once you are abused, once your self-worth is diminished, it starts you on a downward spiral. This book helps you to understand what happened and also helps you evaluate how the people in your life could have helped you and how you can help others. While I wasn't the victim of sexual abuse as a child, not understanding how the world works lead me down a dark path of allowing myself to be used by men in order to try and gain their love and attention. Educating my own children on the value of sex through God's plan of mutual love, respect, and commitment is very important to me. This study encompasses all of that while also allowing for the necessary self-reflection. Why did I allow myself to be treated that way? And how can I prevent my own daughter (and other young women) from ever experiencing that same wretched course?"

Melinda Martin, MusingsOfAMinistersWife.com

TOPICS

HOW TO USE THIS BOOK

Prayfully read each verse before starting each individual chapter. Read through each chapter and spend some time answering the *Rooted Wisdom* questions at the end of every chapter. If at any time you are in need of additional services, please consider the following resources available for your use.

- National Domestic Violence Hotline 1-800-799-7233 http://www.thehotline.org/

- National Child Abuse Hotline 1-800-422-4453 https://www.childhelp.org/

- Rape, Abuse & Incest National Network 1-800-656-HOPE https://www.rainn.org/

I have also created a private Facebook group where you can share your story and seek support from others who are being restored from the damage of sexual abuse.

https://www.facebook.com/groups/639658806165983/

CHAPTER ONE: CAPTIVITY

"See to it that no one takes you captive by philosophy and empty deceit, according to human tradition, according to the elemental spirits of the world, and not according to Christ."
~ Colossians 2:8, ESV

Feeling his soft skin next to hers as he sleeps, Megan cannot fathom how he fell in love with her - especially after knowing her disgraceful past.

It is impossible for her to understand how she deserved twelve years of marriage, four beautiful girls, and a handsome son.

Being a mother of these amazing kids makes her heart incessantly pound with questions. Will they make wise choices? Will they save themselves for their spouses, guarding the gifts that were only meant to be shared with one person?

She yearns to protect them from every hurt coming their way, in hopes that they never face the heartache she did. Still, God's grace has been such a blessing in Megan's life, from start to finish, especially since sex has been ever-present, making her feel unworthy.

She knows that only He can answer the tough questions that life brings, so she is going to choose not to worry anymore as she lays it all at His glorious feet.

She has learned to put her trust and life in His hands; after all, she is a daughter of the King.

Megan Danes was born into what most people viewed as a loving family.

Growing up as "daddy's girl", she often felt looked down on by her three sisters.

Her older siblings didn't always like looking out for her, as their parents would expect of them. Her youngest sister was usually upset that she was not able to do as much as Megan did.

Since Megan was the favorite, according to them, she typically got her way with just a little bit of eyelash batting pointed in Daddy's direction.

She knew how to work the system because it was evident that he loved her. He peppered her with affection every chance he got. But then again, Joshua was known for being squishy on the inside.

Joshua Danes met, fell in love with, and married Bethany Cunningham in only a matter of weeks. She was his angel. She took his breath away - the sun rose and set within her eyes. As far as he was concerned, nothing anyone could say would change the way he saw her.

Bethany was the single mom of two of the most beautiful little, blonde-haired, blue-eyed ladies he had ever seen. Sure, she had a past but so did he. They both saw through each other's baggage to the beauty within and could not help but fall in love.

Bethany's devotion to him and their marriage made him want to be a better man; she had an unexplainable power over him. For her and her two daughters, he was willing to turn away from his thieving ways.

She was a praying woman with great dedication to her faith. Bethany learned to lean and rely on God. His grace and favor, in the decisions she made for her life and the lives of her girls, was enough.

She spent as much time as she was afforded in church or reading the Bible. Her goal was to try to soak in all the knowledge she could about how to live a godly life. From her quiet time and personal experience, she learned that the only way to make this marriage work was to bring God into it. Joshua didn't really believe that anymore, because he struggled to come to terms with his faith.

Joshua was raised in a Mormon household, which stemmed back for an unknown number of generations. There was an expectation of tradition that went along with being a Mormon and faith had nothing to do with it.

Joshua was the youngest of nine children and definitely displayed the "baby syndrome".

His oldest brother was born in 1910, 25 years before him. He was spoiled by his sisters and taught bad behaviors by his brothers.

The boys were a rough group, spending most of their time gambling and drinking. What they didn't have, they stole from others.

Their example of the Mormon lifestyle was that of a Sunday morning Christian. As long as they were in church on Sunday, what they did during the week was not a big deal.

Most of the time they reminded him of the Wild West gunslingers that he read about in his history books at school. It wasn't uncommon for them to be packing Colt .45 caliber pistols tied to their hips.

Growing up in the 1920s, most people lived that way, despite the gun restriction from Congress in 1927.

Their morning encounters were flooded with the hustle and bustle of neighborhood friendliness. They experienced the type of politeness that was only present by pushovers who were too meek to stand up to anyone, let alone the Danes boys.

During the day, they would pickpocket random people and rob the postal service, knowing their safes were not well-cared for. They were quite good at what they did, and due to their demeanor, no one was willing to confront them. It gave them great freedom.

The evening, though, would bring about a different kind of thrill, full of dangerous, sometimes even life-threatening, risks.

The night life was a different group altogether. It was overrun by violent, hateful people that the morning crowd avoided at all costs, feeling quite natural to them. The boys felt an immense rush being around like-minded people, not feeling the slightest bit out of place or uneasy about their surroundings.

This was who they were and where they belonged, like a Southern Baptist preacher at a week-long revival.

Joshua's brothers would gamble and drink away what they stole - at least most of it. In their minds, this routine made it easy to get up the next day to do it all over again.

Since they had only enough money left over to help support the family each evening, there wasn't any cause for explaining what they were up to.

This setup was a perfect combination for them to continue down the path they were on. The daytime folk were too afraid of them to turn them in. The nighttime folk were too excited, seeing their money coming into the games every day to rat them out, even to their own mother.

To their mama, they looked like good, young men.

Her sons would get up early to do chores around the farm, like milking cows, mucking the stalls, feeding the stock, mending fences, repairing any damaged equipment, or shoeing the horses. Of course, they stayed out late at night to "work" at what she believed was a normal job.

They behaved as any normal farming family would. They rotated responsibilities so everyone did their fair share and then off to a formal job they would go.

She was too busy tending to all the younger children to pay any attention to what people were saying about her boys. An overabundance of things to do left little time for their mama to partake in idle chitchat.

Sadie was not a naïve or a socially ill-equipped mother. On the contrary, she was quick as a whip. She was just not the type to sit around and sip tea while hearing the latest gossip from the church busybodies.

Their mama was not one to let a wrong-doing slide by, though. If she discovered any of her children had done wrong, she moved in breakneck-speed to tan their hides with a switch of their choosing.

Mind you that they chose well, so they had to be creative about hiding their real ventures.

Joshua's parents were lenient with him, more so than they were with any of his siblings. His sisters did their fair share of parenting to try to make up for the deficiency. The ladies managed to give him plenty of things to do throughout the day. It was the only way to keep him distracted from wanting to run off with his brothers, something he desired greatly.

The girls taught Joshua how to knit, sew, mend, cook, and clean. They also reviewed his school assignments with him each afternoon. For the most part it worked, but not for lack of trying on Joshua's part.

He made the task of raising him quite difficult. He would find new ways to make messes or break things that his sisters would have to tend to so he could slip away.

He didn't really think his brothers were doing bad things, just exciting things that he wanted to be a part of. When they would ask him to be a lookout or snatch someone's wallet, he would willingly partake.

To his brothers, he was seen as the perfect scapegoat because he would get into little or no trouble. Due to the cuteness factor of his youth, even when Joshua was innocent his brothers still pointed the finger in his direction. He didn't mind, proudly taking the fall for his idols. After all, they did this every day of the week and were still permitted into church on Sundays. It couldn't have been all that bad.

Joshua learned quickly the jobs that needed to be done so that he may live the life he worshiped in his brothers.

Upping the stakes by robbing federal property, rail yards, and people's homes made him big time. The money he stole would go to smoking, drinking, and gambling but the property was another thing entirely.

He began to be bored with the lifestyle so he fashioned himself into a real life Robin Hood, stealing from the rich to give to the poor.

He would seek out property that he believed friends and family members needed or would love to have, steal it and then deliver it to them as a gift. Of course he was smart about it, only gifting them for the holidays or birthdays so no one would see through his lies.

He stole everything that he thought could be useful or bring about a smile to someone else's face. There were dresses for his mama and his sisters, guns and Bowie knives for his brothers, chest of drawers and cedar chests, toys for his nieces and nephews, and food to feed his growing family. Joshua even went as far as stealing to help out neighbors. If someone was in need, then he was there to the rescue with a plow and seeds for a farmer and gas for the preacher's old Model T Ford so that he could go check on his parishioners and witness.

He was so good at what he did. Most everyone, except for his brothers, believed he had a great paying job as an assistant to an attorney. Those who didn't believe knew to keep their mouths shut.

By the time his parents caught on to his outlandish behavior, it was too late.

They had already lost their innocent boy to a lucrative life of crime, coupled with an intimidating personality and a body to match. No one, not even his family, wanted to challenge him. By all accounts, he was a kind person and extremely protective of his family, even if it meant going against them.

In Joshua's mind, his stealing was his way of providing. It wasn't important that he got a rush of excitement doing it, just that it was done. They would want for nothing, which sometimes meant he needed to be aggressive to get his point across.

It didn't take long for things to change.

By the ripe old age of eighteen, the police considered him a person of interest in nearly every robbery case they were investigating. They watched him intently, desperate to catch him in the act, which only gave him a different kind of rush. Adrenaline constantly coursed through his veins at the thought of being caught.

They were unable to pin him down to anything noteworthy. He was, however, a required guest in county jail for a short time just as a warning because the authorities did not have enough evidence to hold him long-term. In that time, his reputation for being a force to reckon with was increasing dramatically.

Due to a stick fight he encountered in the jail yard, fear of him continued to rise. A man stabbed Joshua's neck with a butter knife. The man swiped it if from his lunch tray, all because Joshua did not see color amongst the other guests in county jail, unlike his assailant.

He was swift in his recoil when he flattened the man with one punch. The blow went to the bridge of his nose, while Joshua held his own throat wound closed.

That one act of violence solidified his authority over those who, at one time or another in his life, wanted to test him.

Joshua's life of crime was temporarily put on hold for an involuntary enlistment into the Army. He was called to active duty against Korea in January of '53. He did as he was told, because in war there is no other way to survive but obedience. He fought not for the love of his country but for the need to stay alive so he could return home one day.

He discovered that fear is a powerful ally. Having seen his comrades in arms fall to enemy fire all around drove him to be suspiciously alert of his surroundings and those who were in them.

The fighting only lasted about seven months. This gave him the opportunity to return home but not as a changed man with a softened demeanor. He returned as some tend to do when faced with death--with an untrusting but ever-diligent heart.

Joshua picked up right where he left off the moment he was returned. Only for a brief time did he go unnoticed.

Soon after his return, the FBI got involved.

He was becoming more daring with his federal encounters. In 1959, he was caught with a United States Postal Service safe filled with cash. He served eighteen years in penitentiaries, alongside some of the most dangerous criminals at Illinois State Prison and Arizona State Prison, like Roger Touhy. There he learned new skills from reading the books provided by the prison libraries.

He loved to read law books in an effort to uncover a loophole out of his current confinement. Construction and demolition books were great for discovering how things went together. He even read cook books to aid in his KP duties in the cafeteria. Reading helped him pass the time, since his family only visited on a rare occasion.

Many nights, he mulled over how much he loved his family, especially his mama. There were dozens of times he thought he was a disappointment to her. One thing is for certain--he never doubted the love she had for him.

Her love was spoken in volumes through the affection she showered on all of her children. She had an enormous but tedious routine she completed each day around the house without so much as a furrowed brow. Even the discipline she instilled on them displayed her love and desire for their well-being.

He saw first-hand what love and hard work looked like when watching her care for her family. It was Sadie's example that made it easy for him to dote on his cell mate's family when they came to visit.

Joshua's cell mate, Don, had been recently divorced. He is an odd sort of fellow, Joshua often thought to himself, though he could never figure out why. It helped his days pass by quicker to have someone to talk to. Being cell mates gave them plenty of time to get to know one another, enough that Don regularly invited Joshua to his family visits. Don had weekly visits with his daughters and ex-wife, Bethany. They would come for hours at a time.

While Don would discuss parenting stuff with Bethany, Joshua would play Tic-Tac-Toe, Checkers, or cards with the girls. His job was to keep them entertained and occupied. But when Don played with his girls, Joshua would talk to Don's ex.

Since she was really only there to help cultivate her daughters' relationship with their dad and they came for hours at a time, she had some time to kill.

It wasn't long before they established a great bond. When the time came for Joshua to get released, Bethany, Don's ex, was all too happy to be the one to meet him at the gate.

Because they had just met, it seemed to others that they didn't really know each other. Bethany and Joshua felt magnetically drawn to one another, unwilling to be apart.

He introduced her to his family. Without a moment of hesitation, they ran to Las Vegas, Nevada to make their new life official on April 21, 1977.

They were simply dressed and had just one of his sisters as a witness, but it couldn't have been more perfect.

Joy filled does not even come close to describing how Joshua's heart swelled when Bethany told him they were pregnant with their first child.

He had never experienced this overwhelming emotion before and couldn't get enough of it. Joshua was excited and nervous all at the same time. Throughout Bethany's pregnancy, while caring for her, he couldn't help but worry about his abilities as a father. He recalled all the disastrous behaviors and activities he indulged in and wished his baby would not live the same life.

He vowed to keep his past a secret, hoping its negativity would not rub off on his future children.

Due to his concerns, his 32-year old wife was treated like a queen. He, age 43, placed her on a pedestal in an effort to protect his pride and joy that was growing inside of her. He waited on her hand and foot, making sure she wanted for nothing. Daily he tried to find ways to make her feel more comfortable. His deepest desire was to lessen any displeasure she may be experiencing.

Bethany felt blessed. She knew God had sent her more than just a blessing in Joshua Danes. He was an actual, honest to goodness, visual of God's love for her.

A few years after their first daughter Megan was born, their second daughter Jessica arrived. Their family was complete.

He spoiled all four of the girls. Bethany's older girls were only ever treated like his own, even though they no longer lived with them. He was always proud to be the father of four precious beauties. He wanted the very best for them, and to him that meant steering them away from danger and poor choices.

Joshua worked harder than any man Megan had ever known. When he wasn't at a job site, he was deliberate in repairing or re-modeling things around the house. This was his attempt at making his ladies' entire environment a cozy experience.

Megan's mother went back to school for the purpose of assisting in the support of their family. Her father took on any side job he could find, often several at a time.

Joshua would leave before the sun rose and did not return until well after its setting. He discovered an honest day's pay was much harder to come by than a dishonest one. His old life of crime was in the past where it belonged. He thought to himself, I must do everything in my power to prevent my girls from following in my footsteps!

The sore achy stiffness of his aging body was acceptable to him. In exchange for a family to come home to, he was willing to be in physical anguish.

From his experience, it would have been so easy to dive back into his old lifestyle. He would have been able to provide for his family with very little effort but made a promise to himself not to let Bethany down.

He wanted to be the best provider he could be. Doing that now meant that he had to follow the rules of society. He was hoping to set a better example for his girls than what was provided for him by his siblings.

His mother's love gave him the frame work for how to do just that, all the while displaying love for his wife.

There was no other person he trusted and respected more than Bethany. She had amazing integrity, living up to everything she said. She never let anyone down.

Joshua never really protested anything Bethany said because he knew her heart. He also knew she would not suggest something without great consideration of the pros and cons. She spent a great deal of in-depth time in prayer, asking for the Lord's guidance with every decision she faced.

He supported each decision his wife made, even when she was unsure. He bathed her with encouragement because he understood the vast details she stewed over.

Bethany felt a call to the medical field.

God was ever faithful to point out how compassionate she was towards the hurting. Although she was no longer the age of the average college student, she obeyed His call.

When her nerves got the better of her, Joshua declared, "Honey, you will be forty years old, with or without a college degree so you might as well get one."

He was proud of her. She was doing what he never had the courage or, he thought, the abilities to do himself. His constant support was everything she could have asked for to see her way through the unknown.

Nursing school was a big challenge for Bethany.

She was a good student in grade school but that was many years ago. She struggled with spelling, memorization, and anything pertaining to Language Arts. However, she excelled pretty significantly in Math and Science while in college.

Bethany spent a great deal of time - when not doing the everyday life stuff - locked away in her bedroom studying. The only way of not feeling defeated on this path was to study every chance she got.

Trying to connect her education with her motherhood, she would have her daughters help her study. They would spend hours quizzing her with flashcards. They were not the best study partners but were willing to help anytime she asked.

The girls were always excited to spend this special time with her because she explained they would be a big help. The girls took that very seriously, believing that without their help, their mama might not have ever finished school.

Getting her education needed to be a slow pace for her since she still had to babysit kids in her home to pay for school. What should have only taken a couple of years took nearly four to complete. She knew it was still worth it.

When the day finally arrived when she could walk across the stage to receive her degree, she was thrilled. No one cheered louder than Joshua who beamed with pride at his wife's accomplishment.

She was finally a Registered Nurse, the first in both of their families to graduate with a degree.

She didn't automatically start making the kind of money needed to quit her babysitting. She needed to establish herself as a nurse, so like Joshua, she was doing double-time in the workforce.

During the day, she babysat the neighborhood kids while their parents went off to their nine to five jobs. However, in the evening, after her girls went to bed, she went in to the hospital for the surgical graveyard shift rotation.

It was exhausting.

This routine went on for a few years as they scrimped their way through life but their girls never felt the hardship. Both she and Joshua wanted normalcy and routine in their family, so they made every effort to provide it for their kids.

They spent their vacations camping and playing board games for family entertainment. The girls' favorite past time was watching their parents dance in the living room nearly every evening before bedtime.

Although they seemed to be extremely busy with work, they still managed to share these sweet moments together, with their girls as their admiring and captivated audience.

Jessica and Megan would laugh hysterically at the site of their mom bopping around like her feet were on fire. Just as humorous was their daddy perpetually scratching his feet, one after the other like that of a chicken during their boogie across their small living room floor.

From her viewpoint, Megan thought life could not be any better.

ROOTED WISDOM:

- Megan batted her eyelashes to get her way which is a form of manipulation. Describe a time when you used someone's affections towards you as manipulation.

- Joshua believed he was being a good person by giving others the things they needed, even though he stole them. The chapter listed two neighbors he assisted. What do you think he could have done differently to help them instead of stealing what they needed?

- Look up Philippian 4:6-7, 19 | Matthew 6:25-34 | I Peter 5:7 | Proverbs 12:25. What does the Bible say about worry? Spend a few minutes jotting down a prayer to the Lord, giving Him your worry.

- Joshua found it to easier to sin than live a godly lifestyle. Write about an experience you had where sinning would have been the easier route but God called you to greater things.

- Do you have a Bethany in your life, someone who listens to the Lord and you see His wisdom flowing out of them? If so, take her out for coffee and ask that person to be your mentor.

- Have you ever had to accomplish a task that seemed way out of reach? If so, how did you handle it?

- Look up I Corinthians 9:24. What ways could you challenge yourself more "to get the prize"?

- Why do you think that some people who are raised by good people with the best of intentions can still make morally wrong decisions? Find a Scripture verse that explains your thoughts.

- How do you think being in church could have helped Joshua and Bethany?

'

CHAPTER TWO: CHANGE

"For if you truly amend your ways and your deeds, if you truly execute justice one with another, if you do not oppress the sojourner, the fatherless, or the widow, or shed innocent blood in this place, and if you do not go after other gods to your own harm, then I will let you dwell in this place, in the land that I gave of old to your fathers forever."
~Jeremiah 7:5-7, ESV

As the years went by, it became clearer to Megan how much she did not know about life. Her view was quite a bit more sheltered than she originally believed it to be. Due to her parents' heroic attempts at normalcy, she was not aware of society's desire to keep up with the Jones'.

At school, her friends all had new toys, they never wore second hand clothing, and they ate cafeteria food.

Most kids her age got to go to all the classroom outings or birthday parties. They lived in fancy houses with porches, more than one vehicle, and a treehouse in their backyards. They all seemed to have a picture-perfect lifestyle, one you would see on the cover of a Better Homes and Garden Magazine.

Megan's world was quite different with her Goodwill clothes, sack lunches, and dumpster-diving for anything that the family could use. None of these activities seemed bad to them. In fact, every now and then she and her sister would come across brand new dolls, tea party dishes, and Golden books during their dumpster excursions out in the local landfill.

However, Megan was often left out of activities other girls attended because they did not see her as an equal.

Her classmates did not struggle in school as she did. Grade after grade, she was placed into remedial reading, due to her slow comprehension level. Coupled with stuttering when she was called on to read aloud, she looked stupid to her peers.

She was often called retarded.

Since her reading was so poor, it made all of her other subjects extremely difficult to understand.

She just did not fit, always feeling as though she were the odd man out. She was seen as a lower class citizen.

Megan could recall a time when her peers wore store-bought cut-off shorts that folded up at the thighs. After begging her mom for days, Megan's version was a pair of her old blue jeans cut-off at the knees and unevenly folded up her thighs.

Her classmates saw right through that fallacy and so began her friendship with boys, since fashion was not their thing. It was so easy to make friends with the male species. Everything about them seemed to be beckoning for her attention.

They didn't care what clothes she wore, did not talk behind her back, and included her in every conversation.

She gave them female attention by doting on them, showing complete interest in anything they thought was interesting. Never desiring to ask how they were feeling about things or what they were thinking. None of that mattered to her.

She just yearned for equality in friendship, to no longer be looked down on.

She was even willing to give up credit for a project she completed by herself when she was paired up with a boy, just to ensure his friendship.

The class was assigned a project on weight and density in Science. Megan was paired up with Daniel, the most popular boy in her class. All the boys wanted to be his partner for the coolness factor, and the girls wanted to be his partner for the crush factor.

She drew the short stick, as it were.

Their instructions were to fashion together a floating device that would hold as much weight as possible. No matter the weight, when it was placed in water it would not sink.

Each pair was given only one sheet of a one foot by one foot square of tinfoil and a bag of twenty-five marbles. The teams were instructed that they only had the weekend to get together with their partner to work on it and that no other materials could be used.

Friday came and went. Saturday came and went. Sunday came and went. Megan finally decided to call Daniel to see if he was ready to work on the project with her. "I don't have time to play with you. You do it for us or we will get an 'F'," demanded Daniel.

She felt defeated because she was already struggling in most of her classes.

Megan stared at the foil for hours because she couldn't wrap her brain around this daunting task. At six-thirty in the evening, Bethany told her it was time to take a bath and get ready for bed. She haphazardly placed the foil and bag of marbles on the floor as she stepped into the tub.

Tears began to cloud her vision as she remembered her mother praying for help for everything. She wasn't sure how to pray, what to pray for exactly, or even if He was willing to listen.

She sat there silently, thinking her prayer of desperately needed help, feeling partially silly and partially hopeful. As she was trying to figure out how to remove this burden from her thoughts, a vision of a fishing boat came to mind.

"Boats carry heavy equipment across water all the time without sinking," she deduced.

It may seem like an obvious thing to most but she felt as though she had solved all the answers to the world's biggest questions. A soothing calmness filled her heart so she picked up the tools and began to fold the foil into a makeshift boat.

The water was beginning to get chilly and she hadn't yet bathed, but she was determined to prevent her vessel from sinking.

After several attempts at creating a water tight shape, the first marble went in without taking on any water. Her face was flushed with excitement. Marble after marble went into her ship without it sinking into the abyss of the tub. Finally, she, ran out of marbles. It had worked! Megan was so ecstatic that she reenacted it a dozen more times just to make sure it would hold.

A knock on the door jolted her back to the reality of being in an acutely cold bath. Joshua hollered, "Move it, young lady! You have been in there for over an hour and you still haven't done your homework. Your homework is more important than anything right now. I want you to grow up better than I did."

He was always on her case about being better than he was, but she never truly understood why. She was his daughter, not just somebody's and she thought he was great at being a father. He was like any other dad, normal, so what was the big deal about how she would grow up?

"Oh, Daddy, I just finished it," she merrily shouted back in disbelief, as she scrubbed the dirt off of her body with the frigid water she was lying in.

Monday morning, she and Daniel promptly presented their project to the entire class.

Marble after marble went into the boat until their entire bag was used. The teacher had to add an additional bag, but the space in the boat was now gone and it still hadn't sank.

The class watched in awe as they removed the marbles and started putting gram weights into it instead. The class began counting as each was added, ten, twenty-five, fifty, seventy-five, one hundred, two hundred fifty, five hundred, one thousand grams until finally, at two thousand grams, the boat finally plundered to the bottom of the fish tank.

No one could believe what they were seeing. Someone yelled out that they must have cheated. Their teacher took apart the boat and measured the size of the tinfoil to verify that it had been in fact only a square foot in diameter.

Each student got the chance to examine the flattened foil themselves before agreeing unanimously the validity of their project.

The class cheered for Daniel. The teacher knew better, but said nothing in Megan's defense.

Megan felt that if she tried to correct them, they either wouldn't believe her or she would lose his friendship. She kept silent and was just grateful that her prayer was answered beyond what she believed to be possible.

Not one of the other teams even came close to the four plus pounds they managed to carry in their water resistant craft. In truth, most didn't so much as make it past the first twenty-five marbles.

Daniel let her keep the Science poster of the planets the teacher awarded them with. The class again cheered for his kindness.

This one event manipulated Megan into believing her input didn't really matter so long as she felt as though she mattered to somebody in some way.

She developed the skills of a chameleon, changing herself into whatever others needed so she could blend in with them.

One of her many colors were constructed for sports. Although she loved to play volleyball, kickball, baseball, shoot hoops, gymnastics, and tetherball, she did not have the slightest desire to watch anything professional. To her it was a total waste of time that she would never get back. Clearly there had to be so many more active things she could be doing with her time.

The chameleon in her needed to love sports. If she was ever going to have a chance at obtaining friendships with Daniel and his friends, it was a must.

Megan collected baseball cards and could name every team there was in professional baseball. She knew the players well. As for the really great ones, like Orel Hershiser the pitcher for Los Angeles Dodgers, she could even state their stats.

Ever the team player waiting on the sidelines of any sort of sport, hoping to stand in for someone, the guys instantly accepted her. She was one of their own; they didn't see her as a girl but rather just as an extension of themselves.

Megan was invited to the park for catch, went along for bike rides around the neighborhood, and even helped build a "no girls allowed" fort.

Everything seemed great but then something altered her, creating very distinct differences between her and her clan.

At ten years old, she received what she viewed as a great accomplishment. She started her period for the first time and, boy, was she elated!

Although they weren't around much, she looked up to her two older half-sisters, Valerie and Cassidy.

It made sense that she would be proud of this new experience. It represented the coolest teenagers she knew and made her think about being able to go shopping with them, having them do her hair, and makeup the way that they did.

Little did she know what it truly would mean. None of that mattered to her because she was now privy to her view of the grown up stuff.

Megan got to purchase her very first pads. She even changed them often, not because she needed to, but more for the idea of using her newfound rite of passage.

Her excitement did not last long. A few months down the road, the pain of cramps arrived. They gave her a whole new perspective of what she now believed to be a nightmare into her mind.

Isn't it funny how when your body changes, so do your ideals?

Megan no longer thought of herself as one of the guys. Instead, she wanted to be the one the guys wanted. Something instinctive developed in her when her hormones changed.

Since she developed at a relatively younger age than the other kids in her class, the boys were not yet looking at girls that way. They just felt like she was awkward for wearing a bra several years earlier than most.

It was the first time she became the butt of everyone's jokes, and she often felt the sting of a snapped bra strap.

She didn't understand why it was so hard to fit in. She looked like everyone else. The only two minor differences were her breasts and the beginning formation of an hour glass figure. Not a single person accepted her, despite those differences.

The boys thought there was something wrong with her, and the girls were jealous that she was experiencing puberty before them.

By the time the other girls caught up to her growing figure, the boys started to watch the most attractive girls and would make comments about those that would cross their path. Megan was the exception.

To most everyone around her, she was just average in looks, to some even homely looking.

For the first time, it didn't matter that her daddy thought she was the prettiest girl in the world. She began to reconsider his judgment of the situation. Why else would every other person think she was unattractive except for him?

Girls began telling stories about her. Spreading rumors of her doing things with boys gave them great pleasure. Poor Megan wasn't even aware of what those particular things meant.

Being naïve, she tried to be more like the girls who were talking about her. Megan studied them very closely. She would pay close attention to the way they spoke to and about each other, as well as what they wore and how they did their hair and makeup. She even went as far as writing a letter to one of the popular girls, hoping to become friends. She thought writing it in Spanish, the girl's first language, would make all the difference.

She stood in disbelief as the girl shared the letter with all of her friends while they laughed. Unbeknownst to her, the Spanish language is not written the way English language is spoken, so it was obvious to the other girls that Megan had used a Spanish-to-English dictionary to write the letter.

They never even considered the effort she had put into it. Instead, they made fun of her for thinking she could speak Spanish. It was not her intention at all, but that did not matter one bit.

Since she was never really a girly-girl, she didn't understand the ins and outs of girl drama, causing her to make a socially fatal mistake.

One Monday morning she came to school wearing what the other girls were. Or as closely related as possible. She had tried to match their same style of clothing and what she thought was an adequate hairstyle and an appropriate amount of makeup.

The playground erupted with disgusting comments that brought her to tears. Megan was called whore, slut, and tramp. They even spat out some choice words in Spanish that she could only determine from their expressions were not kind phrases. It was just another way to discredit her as a decent human being.

Clearly her efforts were in vain to her on looking peers.

They saw her as a poor trailer trash girl trying too hard to make friends that, in their opinion, she did not deserve.

Pain filled Megan's heart, which was usually surrounded by love from those at home. She had never before felt a broken heart. The anguish was more than she wanted to bear. Why were people so hateful? Why couldn't they just accept her? Did they not understand how they were making her feel? she wondered.

She tried masking her feelings by laughing off the comments. It seemed that no matter the reaction she delivered, they dug into her deeper.

In that moment, Megan remembered all of the Bible stories her Sunday school teacher told her about turning the other cheek, loving your enemies, and that of the Good Samaritan.

She was to rise above, like the examples told to her. How could they have looked past the bad people and loved them, even though they were being oppressed by them? No way could any of those stories ever have been real. People just don't love those who openly hate them, she thought to herself.

She was called all sorts of names, lied about, and some even threw dirt on her, claiming she should be used to it.

How could people say such hurtful things? Why wasn't anyone protecting her? Why weren't her so called friends sticking up for her?

Sure, Jesus was tough enough to take this. He was God, after all. She knew in her heart she did not have the strength to endure as He did. She knew none of those questions would be answered. Instead, she began to create a wall around her heart for her own protection.

If no one else was going to protect her, she needed to take matters into her own hands and that meant putting distance between herself and the source of her pain.

She kept to herself. Having no friends to hang out with, she just went straight to school and straight back. Recess time was spent sitting as far away from the general population as possible. Megan lived in fear that she would have to endure ridicule if she got close to any peers or played on the playground.

A couple of months later, she went to a slumber party at the house of one of her only remaining friends. Having never before experienced an honest to goodness slumber party, she was blown away by the invite and took a chance in going.

The following Monday morning at school while in the girl's restroom, a fellow classmate noticed bugs crawling around in her hair as she was washing her hands. The classmate excitedly told everyone she came in contact with. The gossip spread like a bad infection, sucking her into the life of a leper.

Megan had no idea what lice were or how she could have gotten it, except from staying the night at the friend's house. No one would listen to her. Adding insult to injury, even her so called friend would not acknowledge her presence.

The school nurse sent her home for treatment. She contemplated telling her parents how the kids at school were treating her, but she was not sure it would have done any good. Her mother would just remind her to be the bigger person and ignore them. Her dad may have thought she was acting like a baby. He would have most likely asked, "Did you do something to egg them on?" And then remind her not to get into any fights, lest she turn into him. That made zero sense because he was a big ball of mush most of the time.

There was no way out of the pit she had landed in. She didn't see anyone coming to rescue her and, clearly, her "lions' mouths" weren't shut by this God people spoke of.

All she could do was wait out the rest of the school year. Since her parents moved frequently, there was hope she could start fresh again in the fall.

A few years passed before she started to trust her peers again.

Even though she had attended a couple of different schools since the lice incident, she was struggling to connect with anyone in her classes.

Depression was beginning to circle overhead.

She spent lunch hours walking around the school field by herself or in the library. Snacking on chips or some other junk food she managed to shove in her backpack in the morning was her way of avoiding acknowledgement of others.

Her bitterness, however, was extremely noticeable to those who she did come in contact with. Poor Bethany was beside herself, unsure of how to fix this child before it was too late.

Joshua and Bethany would plan outings, encourage her to make friends, and visit relatives as often as possible. Their idea was to give the girls, especially Megan, an opportunity to play with others, but none of that really worked.

They were sick with worry. They just kept seeing Megan disappear into herself, becoming less and less socialized.

Once again, time for a change of scenery, thought Joshua. Since Bethany was applying for jobs all over the country, it would be the perfect opportunity to start fresh. Her quest led them to the small, blink-and-you'll-miss-it town.

Bethany's older girls had long moved out. They were beginning families of their own. By the time they decided to move, there was no reason for them to worry about what the older girls thought about the new environment.

It wasn't much of a problem for the younger girls. They were happy to go anywhere so long as they were with their mom and daddy. In fact, Joshua usually made any trip into some sort of adventure.

He loved to take back roads, which were barely visible and sometimes not even present on any map. He loved just to see what would happen or where the road would take them.

On many occasions, they would come across ghost towns to explore that had two hundred year old grave sites. They would eat at cafes out in the middle of nowhere. They were operated by people who looked as though they didn't know what a health code violation was but that was just fine for their trips. They typically would end up on long stretches of open highway, which seemed to never end and had no other cars in sight. Those same roads were usually the ones where they broke down or blew a tire on.

Upon the arrival into this new town, they noticed it was extremely small in size but large in demeanor.

Once things got settled, the family began going to church. Megan felt the sting of judgmental eyes whenever she walked into the building.

Who were these people and why did it seem they knew her a great deal more than she knew them? It wasn't just at church that she felt like an outcast; Junior High was not any different.

Her peers began spreading rumors about her. Being the new girl made Megan an easy target.

Tension rose in her shoulders and arms, tingling all the way down to her finger tips when it was time for each new day. The closer she walked to the school, the tighter her muscles became.

Months went by without any prospects of a friend in sight. Thanksgiving and Christmas were spent alone. While everyone else enjoyed watching the only movie playing at the one picture cinema, hanging out at the Dairy Queen, or bowling at the local lanes, she spent her holiday stuck indoors playing Nintendo.

No one wanted to have anything to do with her; the few times she tried to casually hang out where everyone else was, they would leave when she arrived.

Once a week she could go see the weekly movie but it was easier for her to attend on a Saturday afternoon when the elderly crowd usually watched. She did attempt to go on a Friday night during Christmas break and saw the movie. When it was over, some teenage girls that were two grades ahead began throwing rocks at her to chase her off.

It seemed to her that no matter where she was in town, she was either being stared at with distrust and disgust or ignored and avoided like the plague. It was nearly Spring Break, and Megan was miserable.

One afternoon a girl approached her while she was sitting alone on the track and field bleachers, "Megan, would you like to come over to spend the night?"

Fanny was not the most popular person in school but she knew everyone and knew how to get things. This was the first time anyone had ever acknowledged her. Up until this point she was sure no one even knew her name.

She was astounded by the question and taken aback for a moment. And even though Megan spotted Fanny's two-faced, wheeler-dealer attitude right way, she did not care. In that moment, she knew that beggars couldn't be choosers, and Megan needed all the friends she could get. It was her chance to help balance out the negative feelings people had about her.

Her parents were very glad to see her get out of the house because she hadn't really gone anywhere since they moved. They were so surprised that she had made a friend that they gave her permission to go. She packed an overnight bag and walked to Fanny's.

The town they lived in was divided into three classes of housing. The houses on the hill were where people who could pretty much afford anything lived. The fixer-upper houses near Main Street were where all the adults living in the household had a job and spent any remainder of their income after bills repairing or renovating their house. And finally there were the "tracks", which were shanty type houses located on the south side of the train tracks that housed the extremely poor people, alcoholics, and drug dealers.

Megan lived in a fixer-upper while Fanny lived on the hill, about two miles away from each other.

Megan rang the doorbell and was greeted right away by four Chihuahuas who were anything but friendly. Fanny invited her in and quickly went over the house rules. By the list she was prattling off, Megan could tell the women in that house ruled the roost. There were locks on cabinets, the refrigerator and an outrageous amount of them on each of the bedroom doors.

"Why are there so many locks?" Megan questioned Fanny.

"My older brother sleep walks and steals things in the middle of the night so my mom put locks on everything," she stated with a nonchalant tone.

Megan couldn't help but feel a little uneasy about how common it seemed to lock everything and everyone up in their house.

As they continued their tour, Megan noticed all the Catholic relics drenching their walls, tables, shelves, and even in the bathroom.

"Are y'all Catholic?" she inquired.

Fanny smiled and boldly stated, "We are a deeply religious family." Then with a whisper of a voice continued, "At least that is what my mother says but I'm not sure I believe all that stuff. I really only do the prayers they tell me because I am afraid I will get into trouble if I don't, and my grandmother can be really mean."

Fanny quickly glanced around, surveying the house to make sure no one heard her and went on with the tour. They finally entered her bedroom, which was decked out in pink princess stuff.

Not sure I saw Fanny as the princess type, Megan thought.

Fanny was the only girl and had five older brothers, and she was treated as such but she really didn't look the part. She typically wore a tank top, jeans with holes in them with leggings underneath, and Converse tennis shoes. She did cake on the makeup, wear oversized hooped earrings, and not one hair on her head was ever allowed to stray from the do that she sported.

One of Fanny's older brothers was extremely popular. By association, her brother Javier's popularity made it easy for her to fit in with the in-crowd, because they didn't want to lose his favor.

Javier was the best dancer at all the school dances, learning the latest moves from MC Hammer's "Shuffle" to breakdancing like Michael Jackson.

Everyone wanted to be his friend and hung onto his every word, waiting for his acceptance.

To Megan, he seemed okay but she still did not understand why people put so much weight into what he did or said; he was just another kid.

He did not seem to be a problem, but Megan had a sneaky suspicion this friendship with Fanny was not a wise choice. The friends he hung out with could cause problems if they knew Megan was near him. She ached to have someone to talk to, eat lunch with, and hopefully begin to be able to feel some sort of normalcy so she didn't care what others thought.

ROOTED WISDOM:

- Recall a time in your life when you felt out of place. Was it easier to be who you were or change to blend in?

- Describe a time when God answered your prayer greater than expected and how that made you feel.

- What are some other ideas Megan could have tried to help promote a friendship with her peers?

- Describe a time when you felt defeated.

- Read Psalm 34:18, Psalm 30:5, Psalm 55:22, Isaiah 40:28-31. What do the Scriptures say about that?

- Have you ever compromised who you are to feel a part of something?

- Have you ever had a friendship you knew was not good for you but you did not want to give it up? If so, why not?

- How do you think Megan's parents could have helped her through this time in her life?

- How do you think the church could have helped Megan?

CHAPTER THREE: CLEAN NO MORE

"I know and am persuaded in the Lord Jesus that
nothing is unclean in itself, but it is unclean
for anyone who thinks it unclean."
~ Romans 14:14, ESV

D ue to Fanny's status made by the great Javier, heads were
turning in Megan's direction, who had just turned thir-
teen.

Almost overnight, people wanted to know who this new girl Megan was and what was she interested in? What a strange feeling, she
thought to herself while sitting in first period homeroom. People
knew her name and she had no idea how they did. She shrugged it
off and just went about her business.

Fanny and she became fast friends, hanging out every weekend
and most evenings. They didn't live that close to one another, and
Fanny was never allowed to come to her house, so Megan became
very familiar with walking home late at night through alleyways
and passages through the woods. She also got to know Fanny's family very well.

Fanny's parents were rarely seen because they both worked two
jobs. Her brothers did not care to be around any of Fanny's friends
because they thought of her as a geeky younger sister. Her abuela,
however, was always around to care for her.

Everyone seemed to have freedom but Fanny. Her Abuela watched
her like a hawk. She did not trust her to go to another person's

house for fear that "the Devil will influence you through those people,"--her words, not Fanny's.

The only time she was able to get away with anything was when her Abuela was at an appointment, shopping, or in the hospital.

One such day occurred that changed both girls' lives forever.

Fanny had a boyfriend named Bryce. It really wasn't a relationship because the only time they saw each other was during school, in Mass, or during one of her brothers' sporting events. They were in separate grades, but they were able to spend a few minutes before and after school talking and kissing.

On this special day, Fanny told Megan she wanted her to come along to see Bryce. "He had a friend named Robert who she would love," Fanny delightfully said.

"Bryce says he is shy, funny, and I know he helps out at the church all the time," she stated with robust enthusiasm.

Megan had never been on a date, let alone a double date or blind date. She wasn't really sure this was either but was willing to try anything.

She felt she owed her. After all, Fanny had helped her become somewhat close to popular. People were talking to her in the hallways at school and even socializing with her in public. She wasn't willing to lose that feeling of connectedness.

The foursome decided to go hiking in the mountains. After going a mile into the woods, out of ear shot or the visual of another human being, they opted to separate.

If truth be told, they did not opt to separate. The guys just casually went different directions, guiding each girl along, almost as though it was planned that way.

Beforehand, Megan was pulled aside by Fanny. It was meant to be a private huddle, so that she may tell her "I never get to spend any time with him. We are constantly watched and kept apart. All I want is a few minutes to feel his embrace."

"Are you sure you want to be alone with him? You don't even really know him. What about me? I just met this guy," gesturing with a pointed finger into Robert's direction. "Who is he and why would I want to be alone with him? I know nothing about him?"

"He is fine. Why are you so uptight? Nothing is going to happen. His dad is the football coach and his mom is a teacher at our school. You know her---the one that yells her lessons so loud all the classes down B Hall could take her quizzes. He's harmless. Bryce says he has never had a girlfriend because he is extremely nervous to even be near any girls. What could he possibly do? You will probably do all the talking anyways. Ask him about helping his dad out with the varsity team. That will get him talking and keep him occupied. It will only be for a few minutes, I promise," declared Fanny.

Uneasiness fell upon Megan's gut.

Fanny walked in the opposite direction, leading up to what was known in their city as "make out point". As she did, Megan became increasingly more nervous. She tried indicating her apprehension by mentally willing Fanny to not leave. At the very least, she wished her to turn around and look in her direction. Unfortunately, Fanny was too engrossed in Bryce that she never even glanced back in Megan's direction.

Feeling quite awkward, she asked Robert to tell her about the varsity team and what he does to help his dad out.

"Let's go sit over there." Robert was pointing towards a heavily wooded area with a great deal of brush and boulders to maneuver around. He stated matter of factly, "There is a clearing of grass in the middle where we can sit down in to be more comfortable."

Megan followed reluctantly as he led the way. It didn't seem like she had much of a choice, plus Fanny did reassure her that he was harmless.

After climbing over jagged rocks, crawling under spiky bushes, and tiptoeing around mud, they finally came to a beautiful grassy meadow. It was smaller than what she would consider a meadow but just as beautiful as any she had seen in pictures. The view made her feel very at ease. Since she was in a skirt, she sat on her hip with her legs off to the side and rested her weight on one hand propping the rest of her up.

She asked again about the varsity team, trying to cut the tension. Her real hope was to kill time until her friend was ready to leave.

He talked a great deal about the quarterback's rotator cuff injury in last season's championship game. This somehow, oddly enough, turned into how the new Offensive Coach's equipment just came in after being ordered over six months ago. The conversation, if you could call it that, led into talk about the professional teams. Then to what each team's shot was of getting into the Super Bowl. Lastly, what he hoped for his team.

Without a watch on hand to verify how long they had been away, time seemed to be traveling at snail speed. She couldn't be anymore bored if she tried. He was a total snooze fest, but she was taught to be polite. When in a conversation with someone like this, she knew to keep asking questions, acting as if interested.

Before she knew it, absent from any warning, his hand was cupped over her mouth. The weight of his body was smashed into hers. She was crying in confusion, anger, and pain.

Megan felt as though she was looking down on herself. She desperately wanted to stop whatever he was getting ready to do, but her screams were going nowhere.

The louder she tried to scream, the harder it was for her to breathe.

Megan could see Robert hitting her across the face.

"Scream again, and I will hit you harder," he demanded with great authority.

Her whole body trembled. Why couldn't she stop him? He wasn't much bigger than she was. The part of her that seemed to be floating above the horrific scene could not understand. Why wasn't she kicking him in the groin or biting his hand or spitting in his face? The part of her that was violently being defiled was so traumatized that it had no fight left in it. She just laid there, in a coma-like trance.

Millions of thoughts were running through her mind as he held one hand over her throat and another was quickly undressing her from the waist down.

Who would do such a thing?
Why would Bryce think he is a nice guy?
Why would they leave me alone with him?
Why weren't they checking on me?
Was the same thing happening to Fanny?
Was I being set up for this reason?
Is Fanny really my friend?
What I am going to do?
What will my parents think?
Who will believe me?
How can I ever trust anyone again?
What good am I now?

All of a sudden, memories came flooding back into her mind.

Prior to this rape, she had forgotten all about the images that were in the forefront of her mind right now. This wasn't the only time she had experienced this type of betrayal and abuse.

Megan began to recall a time that she was visiting her older sister Cassidy at her and her husband's apartment. Their parents went out of town for the weekend to purchase a used car. She and Jessica stayed the weekend with their big sissy. She remembers being so excited to be there because their apartment complex had a pool. Cassidy promised they would order pizza.

They went down to the pool to swim for a while. Cassidy's biological dad, Donald, met them down there. He had always been a nice guy but would constantly look at them in an uncomfortable way when they swam.

Donald, whom everyone called Donny, invited everyone over into the Jacuzzi. It was quite crowded, but they joined in right beside him. Donny began to slide his hand up and down Megan's thighs and down the back of her bathing suit. She felt so uneasy that she quickly got out and went upstairs to the apartment.

As that memory was fading, another one became all too vivid.

It was a time when she was a small girl playing hide and seek with a neighbor's daughter in her daddy's shed. The girl was only a couple of years older than her so Megan was not afraid to be playing with her. Things began to get worse when the girl took down her panties and forced Megan to play with her "private parts" as her mother called it. She then made her lay down on the ground so she could do the same to Megan. She remembered feeling mad about having a pleasurable sensation, not understanding what was taking place.

Another vision, which made her feel completely nauseated, showed up.

She was five years old, starting Kindergarten, and so excited to be riding a big school bus for the first time. As she was walking to the bus stop extra early so she would be the first in line, a young man pulled her into the bushes. He held her tight as he surrounded her entire mouth with his. His breathe smelt foul like raw onions. The more she tried to pull away and scream, the more his slobber soaked her face.

Slowly a new memory was being forced out of some hidden place in her brain.

She was four years old at her house, but her parents were not home. Instead, they had one of their friend's teenage sons watch her and Jessica. He told the girls it was time for bed, and he was going to take a shower. The kid got underdressed in front of them, sat on their parent's bed, and told the girls to touch his private area because it was "soft like velvet".

Furiously shaking her head, Megan started to come back to reality, losing focus on the memories.

She was mortified at all the things that she just experienced. She felt violated a hundred times over. What seemed like an hour finally came to an end after only a few minutes.

He peeled himself away, with little regards to what had just occurred. As he zipped up his pants he said with a smug smile looming across his face, "Thanks, that was fun," and began to walk away.

Just as Robert was about to slip out of sight, he warned her. "If you say anything to anyone, I will find you and do that again but next time you will be in too much pain to say a word. Oh, and remember, you are only the new girl so no one will believe you My family and I have been here my whole life!"

Megan was mortified. She sat there with fluid running down her legs, trying to decide what to do next. There was nothing around her that she could clean herself off with, so used her panties, dug a hole in the soft mud, and buried them.

Megan took a deep breath. She wiped her face with the underlining of her shirt. She adjusted her skirt. She carefully smoothed her hair back into place as she began to head out of what she no longer viewed as a beautiful meadow. It was now a place of destruction, masked by wild flowers. The flowers looked as though they were laughing at her as they swayed with the breeze.

Fanny spotted her from a distance. With a grateful smile on her face, she hugged Megan and whispered, "Robert just told Bryce you guys got along great. Thanks for giving me some alone time with Robert."

Beside herself, Megan just gave Fanny a half-hearted smile. She really didn't know what to say or how to act. She could see out of the corner of her eye that Bryce and the despicable pervert Robert were having a good little chuckle. She couldn't make out what they were saying. Did Bryce know? she thought.

The rest of the afternoon, not wanting to draw any attention to herself, she walked silently next to Fanny and as far away from that boy as she could get.

Megan's heart and mind were so torn. Her heart was telling her to run for the nearest police station, a public area of any kind, or look around for an adult who could protect her. Her mind was telling her she was crazy. After all, who would believe the new girl? She barely had any friends, was already gossiped about, and was making claims against the coach's son with a track record a mile long of all his good deeds.

At around four-thirty in the afternoon, the group walked past the city courthouse. Noticing the time on the two foot clock on the building, she was able to make up the excuse that she was required to be home by five for supper.

Fanny said she would call her later and waved goodbye as they continued to walk towards Main Street.

Megan forced herself to walk away casually, at least until they were totally out of sight. Once she realized her group of "friends" was no longer in view, she ran as fast as her legs could carry her. They ached and her innermost muscles were seizing. She felt a burning feeling between her thighs, she couldn't stop shaking, and her face felt like she was running a temperature of one hundred five degrees.

Tears were welling up in her eyes. They were on the verge of streaming down her cheeks, making it impossible to see if she was even going in the right direction.

She was so tired, desperately wanting to sit down but willed herself to keep running. She would be home soon.

As she turned the corner to her street, exhaustion rolled in, causing her to slow her stride. As she approached the house, she realized no one was home yet from the store. She was able to slip in undetected, grateful to not have to explain her appearance to anyone.

Megan was unable to shake the feeling of being dirty.

She undressed in the bathroom, totally avoiding looking at herself in the mirror. Humiliation washed over her as she began to play back in her mind the events that took place earlier in that day.

The room began to fill with steam, the mirror fogged, and she stepped into a scolding hot shower.

Surely this is hot enough to wash off the filth, she reasoned. She began scrubbing herself from head to toe, purposefully. She tried to be as gentle as possible over her scrapes from the bushes, friction burns on the inside of her thighs, and tender spots across her face and body that were maturing into soft bruises. She was attempting to get clean.

She was unable to avoid the feeling that her efforts were not good enough. She could still smell the rancid odor of his Stetson cologne lingering on her skin. She scrubbed again and again and again. Her fingers started to be transformed into withered, pruny versions of themselves and her body felt as though it had lost several layers of skin.

The water eventually grew cold, almost icy. She realized she had been in there way too long, indicating it was time for her to get out. After all, she couldn't hide in there forever.

Looking down at the clothes that once covered a pure, undefiled, body, she picked them up. By the tips of her fingers, she squished them into the trash can. She tied up the bag, put on her robe, and carried them out.

Before exiting the bathroom, she couldn't help but take a cautious look around. She called out to make sure no one had arrived while she was in the shower. She proceeded to walk towards the backdoor.

Carefully looking out the window to make sure the coast was clear, she unbolted the door. Megan ran to the dumpster and threw the bag inside. As she raced back, she slammed the door shut and made sure to bolt it up tight.

Megan crawled into bed. Still in her robe, she pulled the covers over her head and went to sleep.

A few times it seemed while she was somewhat asleep that she noticed her mom or dad would come in to check on her. Fully covered by her quilt, a beautiful handmade quilt that the grandmother she was named after made and she only really slept with when she was feeling ill, they didn't spend anytime disturbing her. They occasionally asked if she was okay.

"Fine, just not hungry because my belly is upset," moaned Megan.

"Megan, Fanny's on the phone. She said you guys had a great time hiking today. She wants to talk to you." Bethany hollered from the hallway.

Despair filled Megan's heart, "Tell her I don't feel well, Mom."

She managed to duck everyone's views all weekend. This task was easy since she was mostly staying in bed pretending to feel sick, which was not altogether inaccurate.

The weekend passed, and by Monday morning, the bruises were so faint she could disguise them with a little makeup.

She went about her normal routine at school with accepting and passing notes to Fanny. She knew change was inevitable, just a matter of time.

Megan started to isolate herself from Fanny's in-crowd, ultimately putting a wedge between the two of them. Once again, she was without friends but that was what she preferred.

She still attended the expected outings like church because she couldn't escape everything. Several months into this routine at a Wednesday night service, she made some new friends.

Noticing her displacement, a few older teens approached her hoping she would want to talk. They asked her all kinds of questions from "How old are you?" to "Do you know how to party?"

ROOTED WISDOM:

- Describe a situation you were in that you had a gut feeling you should not be in.

- Have you ever experienced a trauma that triggered memories of a past trauma? If so, how did you handle it?

- Have you hidden away a hurt, thinking that no one would believe you or take your side?

- Read Matthew 28:20; Deuteronomy 31:6; Isaiah 41:10; Romans 8:38-39; Psalm 23:4. What do the Scriptures say about the Lord believing in you and taking your side?

- How could Megan have handled any of this situation differently?

- How could her parents have been more attentive to her needs?

- What advice would you give to these parents if you were outside looking in to help clue them in on her pain?

- What services could the church provide for this family?

CHAPTER FOUR: CONFIDANT

"Better is open rebuke than hidden love. Wounds from a
friend can be trusted, but an enemy multiplies kisses."
~ Proverbs 27:5-6, ESV

The girls were four years her senior, but they did not seem to mind her age. It was as though they took her in as their mascot, since she was only in Junior High and they were High School students.

They didn't make her feel out of place but instead included her in on everything from there on out.

Megan would often spend the entire weekend either at Holly's or Stephanie's house. These girls were two of her nearly-adult friends, and they made it easy not to show the whites of her eyes to her parents for three days. Her parents did not seem to mind her friendship with them because they were members of their church.

She had so much freedom to feel silly, sad, and happy but never lonely.

They talked about boys, mean girls, bullies at her school, sex, drugs, alcohol, and even her disdain for "Aunt Flo's" visit every month.

They were not just friends but her education into belonging. They taught her how to put in a tampon as opposed to wearing what she believed to be a mattress on her butt. They escorted her to the free clinic for a pap smear and birth control pills.

These girls were her vision of being grown up.

If it was bad, they did it and shared their knowledge. It wasn't long before Megan was no longer seen as the mascot but as their partner in crime.

She was included in all of their parties. She smoked, drank, and even mixed drinks for the crowd. She was witness to orgies where people shared sexual encounters with one another, and it was no big deal to see many couples having separate sex in the same room.

The only thing she didn't partake in was drugs. That did not stop her from creating a "line" for someone or rolling a joint for another in between their sexual escapades.

At each new party, there was at least one new guy to hook up with, just as Holly and Stephanie had taught her.

Megan went through boyfriend after boyfriend. The pain in her heart was too much to bear, so it only made sense to her to grasp love any way she could get it. Having felt so ashamed of the rape, she did not feel anyone would believe her or that her parents, especially her daddy, would look at her the same way again.

Since she believed that she would never have his unconditional love again, she felt a void that was unbearable. Joshua was such a good person; he would never understand why his daughter wasn't.

Each new boyfriend brought about a new sexual experience. She allowed them to do as they pleased with her since she felt powerless to stop them.

Having had such a horrific encounter with someone no bigger than she, and yet, being unable to stop him, Megan didn't think any other guy would be different.

After some time, she learned to seek and feel the pleasure that came from her body being entwined with another. Although these boys were nice to her, she went through them like water. None could fill the void she felt.

One afternoon she spotted a "rebel without a cause" out of the corner of her eye. He was everything a parent would hate in a boyfriend.

He drank, smoked, dressed like a member of Motley Crew, and drove a motorcycle. He had tattoos, and she was pretty sure he did drugs but she did not care. He was the first guy that actually "dated" her.

He took her out in public to the movies, restaurants, and to the town parade, anywhere a normal couple would go. He treated her as though no one else in the world mattered. He played music on his guitar for her, danced her around his living room, scooped her up into his cradled arms, stroked her hair, and kissed her passionately. He cared for her, never demanding anything in return, and always considered her feelings above others.

There was gentleness and goodness in him, even if others couldn't look past his tough guy persona.

Tony was a high school junior when Megan was only in the seventh grade of middle school. They had mutual friends, a lot of common interests, and an instant attraction. It wasn't long before they fell into bed together, but he was a gentle lover who spent more time holding and cuddling her than anything else.

She felt safe with him, enough to tell him what had happened to her.

He felt protective of her. Tony would swing by Megan's school every day at lunch to take her to Dairy Queen or on a picnic and then again after school to bring her home.

Since her parents were never home until late he was able to stay and cuddle on the couch. He would read to her while they ate an afterschool snack together and talk.

Soon the short time they spent together was quickly not enough.

She began sneaking out at night, busting out her screen so she could crawl out her window. The first night, Megan left her bedroom window at two o'clock in the morning. She walked in total darkness, as the town completely shut down at one every morning. She crossed the bridge over the railroad tracks to the shanty side of town and walked along the riverside.

In all, it was a three mile trek just to lie beside him.

Tony had a room off the side of his mom's house with a separate entrance. She knocked softly on his door. She was not sure if he would even hear her because he tended to sleep like the dead.

After a few minutes, he came to the door, shirtless and with a warm, inviting smile. Without saying a word, he wrapped his comforting arms around her body, pressing her cheek into his chest and lightly stroking her hair. He led her into his room, pulled back the covers, and tucked in beside her.

They fell asleep.

As the sun rose, he walked her home. He helped her back up into her room and placed the screen back on the window.

Looking at each other, they knew that would now be their new routine.

From that night on, Tony would walk to Megan's house around one-thirty in the morning. He would wait for her to come out and walk her back to his house.

They spent the walk, every week night, holding hands and talking about the future. She would tell him about her day and he would do the same. They discussed family problems, his job, and where they would live. They had been oblivious to the world for six months.

Their nightly visits grew lengthier. Megan was daring enough to even leave her room at ten o'clock at night, not thinking anyone would notice.

At the beginning of Christmas break, someone noticed.

While Megan and Tony were sleeping in his bed, her little sister Jessica woke up from a nightmare and tiptoed down the hall to Megan's room. She was hoping she would be able to sleep in Megan's room with her instead of waking up her parents.

Jessica slowly opened the door, expecting to just slide into Megan's extra twin bed. She stopped short when she noticed Megan's bed was unused. Jessica began to scream, "Daddy! Daddy!"

Joshua ran in the room, nearly slamming the doorknob into the wall to see what was wrong. When he realized what the commotion was all about, he began to question Jessica and Bethany, expecting they knew something.

For six hours, Joshua knocked on every door of the people he knew Megan associated with. He never even took a minute to think about the fact that he was banging on their houses in the wee hours of the morning.

Around four o'clock in the morning there was a rather disturbing knock on Tony's door. Along with it came a thunderous voice on the other end, yelling "HELLO!"

Megan hid in the bathroom as Tony answered the door. She could hear her daddy, the man she admired for many years, yelling in anguish. He accused Tony of knowing where she was, but she refused to come out. She feared that he would see first-hand her reality.

No doubt he would see her as she saw herself--nothing but a disgrace, no longer his daughter.

In her heart, she knew that what she was doing was wrong. Even though Tony treated her kinder than others, she felt uneasy, unsure why.

Megan assumed her dad would never believe her about the rape if she came out of the bathroom right now. If he knew she was in another man's house, she knew he would not believe her. Why should he?

Her head was throbbing with a voice yelling somewhere inside, "WHORE! WHORE! WHORE!"

As Tony closed the door, they both knew that Joshua was just standing on the other end, unable to move.

Feeling exhausted from his search and discouraged by the results, he walked away. He felt powerless.

Neither of them seemed to breathe for what felt like an eternity. When Joshua was finally out of sight, they sat on Tony's bed trying to decide what to do. Their secret was out. Her parents knew she was not home at night anymore, so what were she and Tony going to do? There was no point in hiding it.

As the sun rose in the east, so did the nervous couple.

Tony began to walk her home but Megan left him at the bridge in an attempt to protect him. She encouraged him to let her finish the rest of the journey on her own.

He wanted to be by her side as she stepped back into the house. He wanted to guard her from the pain, but, with sadness in his eyes, he let go of her hand. Tony watched as she walked away, unaware that it would be the last time he would see her.

Turning the knob to the front door, Megan boldly stepped inside her house. She was greeted by her father on the couch and her mother pacing the kitchen.

"Where have you been, young lady? I have been searching for you all night long. Your mother has been worried sick. Answer me when I am talking to you," was Joshua's larger than life demand.

"I know," she said without hesitation and with some remnant of annoyance in her voice.

"How do you know I have been looking for you?" an irritated scowl etched across Joshua's face.

Since she feared the worst if she admitted where she had been, a lie was the only thing she could manage to come out of her mouth.

"I was awake all night walking the alleyways with friends. I stopped at a friend's house and they told me you came by so I didn't see any reason for coming back through the window."

"Whose house? What were you doing, walking the neighborhood? Were you stealing things? Are you drunk? Are you on drugs? Haven't I told you not to turn into who I was? You are not just somebody's daughter. You are mine, and I will not tolerate this behavior." He pressed with disdain and disbelief.

"What the heck are you talking about? It doesn't matter, Dad. Just drop it because you wouldn't believe me even if I told you," she stated, tight-lipped.

With his eyes squinted taut and his face fire engine red, Joshua bellowed, "You are grounded to your room and I will be nailing your screen shut, all the way around your window!"

The doorbell rang midafternoon, and Megan could hear familiar voices coming from the living room. As she walked down the hall, it became apparent who was in deep discussion with her parents. It seemed an odd time for a visit. Considering her sister and her husband lived four hours away and she was unaware that they planned on coming up, she felt puzzled.

Strange that Valerie and her husband Mark smiled awkwardly at me, she thought as she entered the room. Megan brushed it off. "Hi, Sissy, I didn't know you were coming. Are you staying all weekend?"

"No. What do you think about coming and staying with us for a while?" Valerie answered back with an uncertain tone.

"Cool! For the rest of Christmas break? Or will I be back for Christmas morning?" Her question came with joy and relief, thinking it was just what she needed in order to dodge what was sure to be more questioning from dear old dad.

"I don't know what to do with you anymore. I am afraid you will end up like I was as a teenager. I don't know any other way of stopping you from going down this destructive path," despair loomed across Joshua's face as he said those words.

"I don't understand. What are you saying, Daddy?" Megan knew in her heart what he was alluding to but hoped she was wrong with her question.

"Your mother and I have decided to let you live with Valerie and Mark for the rest of the school year. We think if you are away from here that you will make better choices. I just don't want to see you get hurt or in trouble. Your actions lately do not show me that it will happen if you stay here."

"What? Are you kidding me? I can't leave. My friends are here. Please let me at least say goodbye to them," she begged, tears flowing down her face. The only person she could think of was Tony.

She contemplated ways to escape. Run away? Sneak out? Ask her sister for help? She would do anything just so she could see him one last time.

He would know what to do. He could take care of her.

It was too late. Joshua began packing her belongings even before she returned home from being with Tony. Bethany wrote out a note of guardianship for Valerie. In less than an hour, Valerie and Mark were on the road, Megan reluctantly seated in back, aching on the inside.

With a tear stained face, Megan asked, "How did you know?"

Valerie turned her head towards the back seat so she could be as direct as possible with her little sister. "Mom called us at around five this morning, crying her eyes out. We talked for about an hour. You really hurt her, Megan. Then Dad got on the phone and discussed arrangements with us. He said he would pay for gas if we came now and told us they would give us a hundred dollars a month to support you. What was I to say? Why does this even bother you so much? You love coming to our house, and Mom says you haven't been getting along with anyone. You never spend any time with Jessica, either. He said it wouldn't be a problem and that all of your stuff would be packed before we arrived. Dad said to make you feel at home so we have a cool room set up for you. Why are you so upset?"

She chose not to respond. To admit to what had really taken place would mean she would need to admit to lying. So far, she was only thought of as the kid who snuck out. She definitely did not want to be known as a liar and a whore, too.

ROOTED WISDOM:

- Why do you think Megan went through guy after guy?

- Have you ever tried to fill a void with superficially bad behavior? If so, what was the outcome?

- Why do you think Megan felt that it was wrong to be with Tony, even though he treated her so well?

- Do you think Joshua and Bethany should have sent Megan to Valerie's home? Why or why not?

- Read. Ephesians 6:4, Deuteronomy 4:9, I Chronicles 28:9. What do the Scriptures say about parenting?

- Do you think Joshua was listening to God? Why or why not?

CHAPTER FIVE: CORRUPTED

"Be sober-minded; be watchful.
Your adversary the devil prowls around like a roaring lion,
seeking someone to devour."
~ I Peter 5:8, ESV

Her room was set up in the back of the house, which included a stereo, waterbed, and dresser. Mark helped her get settled and Valerie took her shopping for school clothes and supplies. School started two weeks from Monday.

Almost instinctively, the kids in her classes picked on her.

Megan was definitely the minority in a predominately Hispanic school. Aside from her, she only noticed one other Caucasian girl who she later discovered was the principal's daughter.

Her self-esteem was at an all-time low. It was all she could do to mope her way to school every day. It felt as though she was right back where she started from when her family moved to that small town. There was only one difference between then and now--a larger city with more people to ignore her.

She still had no friends and was lonelier than ever.

She spent months building meaningful relationships back in her Podunk town. Bitterness grew and festered inside Megan because of how lonely she was feeling. All those friends were lost when her parents made her leave abruptly. She had none of their contact information and no way of knowing if they knew what happened to her.

The only comfort she received was from her brother-in-law, Mark.

He included her on projects around the house, outings for his work, and fun family activities. Everything seemed normal in the way Mark treated her. She was, after all, his little sister-in-law, so she trusted him.

More and more, Mark pulled Megan into his life. He began sharing his life with her as though they were friends. It felt nice to have someone to talk to.

Without any other friends, she missed intimate private conversations.

Megan began to feel very close to her new family. Valerie would plan fun outings in an effort to help Megan feel normal and loved.

A park visit was never just a park visit. Valerie packed an amazing picnic lunch every time. They brought motorcycles to ride and played tetherball.

Their parents never would have approved of Megan riding a motorcycle all by herself. She managed to crash it and scraped up her leg, but it was the most fun she had had since leaving home.

They frequently went camping and fishing just to get out of town. On one such camping trip, Megan realized her friendship with Mark was not just a simple friendship.

All was quiet at the campsite. Valerie had already gone to bed while Megan was roasting Marshmallows.

"Let's go night fishing," he playfully suggested.

Mark was easy to say yes to. She trusted him with good reason, because he generally behaved as a caring big brother.

They grabbed the poles and lawn chairs and headed towards the lake. "I thought fish slept at night?" Megan inquired.

"Of course, but if we put our poles in now, we will have fish on the line by morning. Let's just bait the line, throw it in, and anchor down the pole before we head back," Mark suggested.

She did as he said and began to turn towards camp. He grabbed her arm and pulled her close to his chest, asking if she felt cold.

Megan shook her head no and felt very unsettled about the way he held her body near his.

As he ran his hands up and down her sides, she knew something was not right. How did she say something without upsetting him? Maybe she was reading more into it than what he really intended. If I say something about it, will he blame me for something? My sister will never believe me. Keep your mouth shut, Megan, she thought.

He kissed her.

Shock ran over her body. She stood there, unable to move. Memories of that afternoon in the woods with Robert lying on top of her came flooding into her mind. Memories of other perverted, twisted people she had allowed to use her followed suit.

Not wanting to feel victimized again, she began to build a wall of lies. This was my doing. I encouraged it. I wanted Mark to kiss me. We are meant to be together. Why else would he choose me over Valerie? The thoughts kept rushing through her mind.

She started to hate herself. Her self-esteem was next to nothing. Even though her heart ached, this was a time when only her brain had a voice.

Daily, Mark would find a reason to be alone with Megan.

Kissing was no longer the only thing he did to her. She knew it was not where he would draw the line, even if she gave him many excuses.

Megan tried to avoid him by busying herself with school functions and homework projects. There were times when she even asked Valerie if she wanted to join them. Nothing seemed big enough to distract him from his desires.

Mark began undressing in front of her, telling her to hold him and touch him. He was gentle with his words, but his expressions and gestures made her believe she had no choice.

He would grab hold of her arm when discussing his suggestions. The force was just enough to ensure there was no other option for her.

Megan gave in and did as she was told. She allowed him to take advantage of her and even managed to play the part of "girlfriend" very well.

At night when everyone was asleep, Megan would sob warm, stinging tears. God, why are you not helping me? I am nothing but a monster, out to destroy everyone. I deserve what I get. No wonder You abandoned me! I thought I was supposed to be your daughter, Father in Heaven? I wish I was somebody's daughter because then maybe I would be protected. All I am good for is pleasing men. I am never going to be loved by my family or a man. Who could ever love me? All I am is a play toy to guys. Is there something wrong with me that makes it okay for them to treat me this way? Where are You? Her thoughts felt unanswered. Megan retreated into the character she had become-- the mistress.

She was deceitful to her sister and herself. Megan piled lies on top of lies to protect her sister from hurt feelings and betrayal. She lied about what Mark and she did together, because she felt responsible for their marriage, wanting to do her best to protect what sanctity there was left of it.

Several months passed with Mark's ever lurking presence. His drive towards her became obsessive. He questioned her about who she would talk to on the phone or why she needed to stay after school. He would be spotted conveniently driving past wherever she happened to be if she was not at home. He had to know her whereabouts at all time.

She tried to become more involved with teens her age. Megan started to hang out with some girls down the street from where they lived and was introduced to Jason. He was dreamy and somewhat familiar with a very flirtatious smile.

One afternoon they got to talking about where they knew each other from. To their amazement, they realized that he worked along-side Mark. Jason was also the son of Mark's step-mom.

Jason thought it was cool that they would be able to get together a lot at family functions. She begged him to spend time with her away from their families.

She believed she finally had an out in this teenage heartthrob.

He kept her distracted from Mark by picking her up after school. He would take her on dates and not bring her home until required.

Her absence seemed to make Mark feel lonely. She hoped it would make him turn back toward Valerie, leaving her alone.

He did turn back but not exactly how she thought it would take place. Mark returned to Valerie's company but only after confessing his intimate encounters with Megan.

He was jealous that Megan was not paying attention to him. Valerie was faithful to dote on him incessantly so he preyed on her codependency. He wanted to punish Megan for hurting him. Mark thought, If Valerie knows, she will hate Megan and then Megan will get what she deserves. Megan will know what it feels like to be all alone.

Valerie fell into a deep depression and told her parents to come get Megan.

Puzzled, they wanted an explanation to the problem. They assumed she had once again resumed causing problems, like sneaking out.

It was far worse than they could have possibly imagined, Valerie explained in hatred.

Joshua was on fire with rage, wanting desperately to report Mark to the police but Valerie begged him not to.

She believed that Mark would change. Now that her parents moved into town and took Megan to live with them, nothing could stand in his way. She also believed that Mark was not at fault, that there was no way Mark would have ever done any of this without Megan provoking him. She believed Megan was the instigator and told her parents such. Valerie was completely disgusted with Megan, stating she was no longer welcome in her home.

The pain that consumed Megan's heart brought thoughts of suicide to her mind. She obsessed over how to kill herself, hoping it would bring some relief to Valerie.

Even though she was only fourteen years old, Megan believed it had to have been all her fault. She spent days reliving every detail of the time she spent at her sister's house.

She tried to find some sort of clue as to what she did to spur him on. The only conclusion was that she was made for this purpose. She was nothing but a thing for men to use. She was so mad at how her life had been developing, and there didn't seem to be a light at the end of her tunnel.

Megan's anger spilled over into her mind. He is a man, she is a kid. Who was supposed to know better here? He is a married man. She is his little sister-in-law who was filled with fear from others' sexual abuse of her. She didn't have the strength or knowhow to fight back. Why was she being blamed? He should be ashamed, and her sister should have protected her. She could hear the screaming in her head but did not have the courage to let it out.

Again, no one would believe her if she chose to stand up for herself. The best thing Megan could do was to let it go and move on. She hoped one day that Valerie would see things clearly and mend their relationship. She loved and admired her sister, and it was miserable being estranged from her.

It was, however, easy to forget about Mark once she started at her new school. Perversion still seemed to follow her, no matter where she was. In any case, high school was much easier to deal with. At first, the students still saw her as an outsider but the boys were intrigued by her worldliness. She was also the only person in her class that had a job.

Megan started working for Mark's sister, June, and her husband, Bob, cleaning their house for five dollars an hour. She had a great time because June would teach her things about horses. She even took her out riding once a month. It wasn't the best job, but it made her a little spending money to goof around with.

One evening after cleaning, they asked if she wanted to stay for pizza and a movie. "Thanks, that would be great." When the pizza arrived, they dished it out, got some sodas, and started to eat. Since the pizza was too hot to pick up, Megan decided she would cut her pizza slice and eat it with a fork. As she stood up from the table to go into the kitchen to get one, she asked Bob, "You want a fork?"

"What did you say?" Bob questioned with a mischievous smile as he thought he heard her say a more exciting four letter word.

"No! Do you want a fork?" Megan's face blushed, not from embarrassment but from rage. All she could think was What is wrong with all these guys to think that all I am is an easy screw?! Are they all this nasty with women? Do any of them think about anything other than that? She was devastated by his inquiry, even if he was joking. She decided it would be the last time she would ever work for them again.

Bethany had enrolled Megan and Jessica into a Christian High School. Megan needed a little Jesus in her life, or so Bethany thought. What better way to accomplish purity than to place her in an environment with purity-driven people? But again perversion seemed to follow her.

What a joke. Within the first week of school, boys were trying to causally touch her. Sure they apologized, claiming they bumped into her by accident. Nothing was further from the truth.

During one of her classes, Megan's teacher paired the students up and then told them to find a quiet place to work on their assignment together. Megan had been paired up with the pastor's son, who said he had the perfect place in mind. While working on an assignment with her in a private area – the attic of the church - he forced himself on her, touching every sensual part of her body and then told her no one would believe her over him.

Was this how it would be for the rest of her life? What was wrong with guys? Why couldn't they control themselves? Why did they treat the really pretty girls like China dolls and treat her as though she was a prostitute? They had a dress code so she wasn't even dressed provocatively. It is not like she wanted the past she had. She certainly didn't flaunt it, but it seemed as though everywhere she went there was a huge target right across her vagina.

Once again, rumors began to spread about her, where she came from, and the fact that she was not a virgin.

How did they know? Why were people, these so-called Christians no less, gossiping about her? Megan wondered if it could even be called gossip when the adult staff were saying things about her. They compared her to a lady named Rahab, speaking under their breath about being a harlot.

Without much delay, she found herself lacking friends again. The girls in the school didn't want to be associated with her, not even her sister Jessica. Who could blame them? People were probably wondering if any of Megan's bad behavior would rub off on her.

The guys, some of whom she thought of as really great friends, were no longer allowed to speak to her, per their parents' demands.

When she had finally regained her parents' trust just after obtaining her driver's license, Megan had had enough of the abuse. She tried explaining to her parents what was going on at school with the other kids. Bethany believed her to be a liar, because she trusted the ladies of the church over her own daughter. They were God-fearing people, so why would they lie? Megan had lied in the past and had not shown any interest in having a relationship with God. She was of no help to Megan, prompting Megan to turn to her daddy.

Joshua's ever-present disappointment was all too clearly posted across his forehead. She knew he stopped taking her side the day she got caught climbing out of her window. She missed him. She wished he would have compassion for her and tell her everything was going to be alright. She wanted to bat her eyelashes to get her way again, but that was not possible.

Since no one would believe her, she just decided to be bad. She recognized she was never going to be good enough for anyone. She was as rotten as people thought. She concluded there was something extremely wrong with her, and all she was doing was bringing everyone else down.

The longer Megan stayed in that school, the more she was seen as the thorn in everyone's side. The teachers avoided dealing with her, sending her to the principal's office just to get her out of their class. The parents were afraid of their teenagers being corrupted by her evil ways. Even the pastors would not allow her to answer questions in class, not knowing what kind of evil would spew from her lips.

Megan began ditching school. With a car all to herself, it was effortless. She just walked right out of class and drove off.

The staff couldn't stop her, and her parents both had jobs so they couldn't prevent it from happening either. She was finally free from being the victim.

When her parents found out she'd been skipping school, they sat Megan down and asked how they could help her be better in school.

Her only response was she was not happy there because no one liked her. She wasn't going back. Knowing that they would not believe her stories, she told them to put her into a public school where she wouldn't cause any more trouble for Bethany's church friends.

They agreed. If that is what it would take to get her to stay in school, that was what they were going to do. Seeing that they had no real way of controlling the situation, they decided to put her into public school.

What was surprising to her was that they didn't even put up much of a fight.

Megan believed it was because Bethany still thought that the church, which ran the school, was her home. She thought Bethany would be embarrassed if she did anything to ruin Bethany's reputation.

It just seemed easier to take her out than try and defend her. After all the problems Megan caused in the past, Bethany probably didn't consider Megan's innocence anymore. The very next Monday, she started her junior year at a regular high school.

ROOTED WISDOM:

- How could Megan's family have helped her through her depression?

- How would you have handled the situation with Mark, Megan's brother-in-law?

- Why do you think Megan thought everyone distrusted her?

- Discuss a time when you felt trapped in a situation and how it made you feel.

- What suggestions would you give to Megan to help her out from under Mark's control?

- What do you think the Bible says about how Megan should have handled the situation?

- Why do you think Megan felt targeted? And do you think she could have done anything to change it?

- How would you feel if you were Megan and your mom chose the church friendships over you?

CHAPTER SIX: CONFUSED

"For where jealousy and selfish ambition exist,
there will be disorder and every vile practice. But the wisdom
from above is first pure, then peaceable, gentle, open to
reason, full of mercy and good fruits, impartial and sincere.
And a harvest of righteousness is sown in peace
by those who make peace."
~ James 3:16-18, ESV

It was grand. She had never seen a school so big. Life felt stupendous because there were so many people to get lost in. Having way too much to do made it impossible for her to feel like an outsider.

Right away, she made friends with some cowboys, stoners, and nerds. At her other schools, these groups would have never associated with each other. No one seemed to care at this school. Everyone just mingled, and she loved it.

Less than a week later, hundreds of people knew her name, saying hi as they passed her in the hall.

Kids were willingly sitting with her at the lunch room table, without her even asking. Notes were being passed to her in the halls as she was on her way to her next period class. Throughout the week, kids were coming to hang out at her house after school. Once or twice a week, people would ask if she wanted to join them for lunch at Taco Bell, off campus.

She enjoyed going to school, especially Navy Junior Reserve Officers Training Corps where she met Ken. He was a total geek but really funny. She could tell right away he was a total class clown, and everyone laughed when he was around. She and Ken got along great.

It wasn't long before Ken began showing up at all of her classes to walk her to her next class.

They talked about everything and played jokes on one another, like a brother and sister would. Several people commented about how well they knew each other. They decided to play a prank on the entire student body in an effort to see how fast news would travel. They became cousins. Not really, but they started the rumor that they were cousins. Ironically, it made it really easy for Megan to fit into groups. She was instantly accepted, being related to Ken.

The truth in their identity remained this way for most of the school year. When they weren't hanging out, she was working. Fixing pizza was part-time job, after school and on weekends, that gave her play money.

Having over a hundred friends was great but quickly became more expensive than she had imagined. It wasn't that she was paying for them to do things. They just always wanted her to join whatever fun thing they were doing if she wasn't at work. Her money rolled out as fast as it came in, since she also had to pay for her car insurance and gas.

Ken and Megan's friendship grew deeper. Going on group dates was real common but it was not yet known by their peers. They liked each other but they were still fake cousins. On Valentine's Day, Ken went out of his way to make Megan feel special.

He toilet-papered her car with pink toilet paper and placed a sign on her car that read, "I love you." He bought her favorite candy and lunch and delivered it to her during her lunch break. He had a candy gram sent to each of her classes.

News of the "kissing cousins" traveled fast. Both of them were bombarded by disgusted looks and questioning remarks. It took some time, but they were finally able to put the rumors or lies to rest.

The word was out that they had masterminded the entire thing. Even weeks later, people were still questioning it, but it soon became old news.

Ken and Megan dated for a while before they became intimate. At first she was reluctant. She knew the pain from all those other encounters could come rushing back to smack her in the face. They talked often about eventually getting married, so it felt like the right thing to do.

He said all the right things about a future with her, which no one else had ever done before. He said he loved her and wanted to spend the rest of his life with her. Only one other person said that but she wasn't moving anywhere this time.

It sounded perfect to be wanted for more than just sex, to be wanted for a lifetime. Plus, it was not like she was a virgin anyway, so what was the big deal? Giving herself to Ken wouldn't matter because she had already been destroyed when someone took away her purity.

Ken Matthews wasn't what some might call handsome, but he was faithful and attentive to Megan. He spent all his free time with her. Longing and lust gripped his insides every time he thought of her.

He had not yet known a woman. There had been a couple of girls wanting to take that from him but he did his best to remain that way. Until he met her.

She never quite figured out what he saw in her but was glad he did. She understood that there must have been something special if he wanted to lose his virginity to her. He made it a point to say that he saved it for the person he wanted to marry.

Megan was not like any other girl he knew. There were so many girls falling all over him. People flocked to the way he took charge of a room but she never did. Girls laughed at his jokes, were always in the places they knew he'd be, and wrote flirty notes to him at school, all day. Not Megan.

She called him to the carpet way too often, saw right through his clown act, and treated him like a kindred spirit.

What an odd sort of person this Megan is, he pondered. She was the only girl who didn't have a desire to pursue him. This behavior made his chase all the more appealing, causing a powerful sexual drive that he did not know how to control. She was never far from his mind. He made every effort to make sure he was not far from hers. Valentine's Day won her over.

A few short months later, they were caught, naked, on the floor in her living room. By her dad.

"Get up! Get Dressed! Get out! I am calling your parents, young man."

A ghostly white complexion fell on Megan's face. She was humiliated and ashamed. Scrambling to cover herself with pillows, the story of Adam and Eve sinning in the garden and then covering themselves out of shame and embarrassment as they tried to hide from their Father flashed in her mind with anguish.

"Please, sir, I love her. I plan on marrying your daughter. I am not just using her. We belong together," he offered as he was being booted out the door by a man three times his size.

The door slammed shut, but no more words were spoken. Her heart was broken but not from how Ken was treated. She was in anguish thinking about how her daddy would see her now. For many years, Joshua had been her hero and all she would be is a disappointment.

She picked up her clothes and ran to her room. Megan could hear the entire embarrassing conversation Joshua was having with Ken's mother over the phone.

She was so mortified that he saw her that way that she tried avoiding contact with him for weeks. Any time they couldn't avoid facing each other, Megan carried her head down low so as to avoid making eye contact with her dad.

When her parents were gone to work one day, Ken pulled up to the curb and Megan hopped into his car. They held hands but didn't speak. He drove her to the parking lot of the mall and pulled into the closest spot he could find, under a shade tree. Neither said anything for such a long time, probably afraid of the other being mad. Would he tell her it was over because his mom said so? Would she tell him she couldn't see him anymore because her dad wanted to kill him?

"This isn't how I wanted to do this. I am sorry we have come to this, but I feel like now is the best time, instead of waiting any longer." Ken reached into his pocket and pulled out a small black velvet, satin-lined box.

She was not even paying attention to his actions. All she could think was Here we go with the goodbye-nice-knowing-you speech. But then she snapped back into reality when he held the box in front of her face.

There is no way this could be what I think it is. I am only seventeen. People don't get married at seventeen. There must be something else in that box because we haven't been dating that long. I am sure he would have said something if he was going to buy a ring, she thought in deep confusion.

"I love you and want to spend the rest of my life with you. I hadn't intended on asking you this way. I had planned on singing to you at our choir concert but the last time we were together kind of put a kink in that plan. Will you marry me?" He prattled off at record speed.

"Yes."

Ken placed the ring on her finger and suggested that they go tell their families right away. He didn't want there to be any hurt feelings, things left unsaid, or festering anger from her dad. He thought this was the best way to achieve that by being upfront and honest right away.

The reaction they received was not at all what they thought it would be.

"Get out. Pack your bags and get out this minute" Joshua ordered.

Bethany just cried.

"Are you kidding me?" Megan questioned in disbelief. She couldn't comprehend why he said that when Ken had done what she thought was the appropriate thing.

He wanted to make an honest woman out of her. He wanted to prove to her father that he had fully intended on marrying her.

She didn't want to "live in sin" as her mother put it, so why were they treating them so badly?

Megan ran upstairs and packed some bags. She took one last look around her room at all of her belongings. Knowing she could not take any of it, she walked out the front door with Ken trailing behind her.

She sat in her car for more than ten minutes. She was secretly hoping one of them would run out to stop her with open arms. She wanted them to show her she was not just somebody's daughter-- she was theirs, protected and loved. Their front door never opened and the curtains didn't even twitch with the hint of someone peeking out. So off they drove, Ken leading the way to his house.

Next on their agenda were his parents. They were not Christians. They were, however, still aggressive with their kids but pretty liberal in their morals and virtues.

He explained that she had been kicked out. They agreed to let her stay in Ken's room and Ken could sleep in the guest room.

His parents were never really settled with the idea of Megan living with them. They made sure to keep her walking on eggshells for the duration of her stay through intimidation.

She and Ken managed to be okay with the living arrangements until tax time came around.

Prom was right around the corner. Ken had intended on taking her to the prom in style but sat her down for a conversation first. Since he was no longer in school, had a good job, and was an adult, he decided it was time for them to be away from everyone.

They were not happy with where they were staying. He knew the attitude his mother was giving her was making things worse by the day. They needed to be out of there, and really, who was going to stop them?

They opted to spend his tax money on a new apartment. Of course, Megan was a little sad at having missed the Prom, a teenager's rite of passage, but this was even better. They moved into a one bedroom within a week and left their families behind. Unaware or unwilling to see the problems that lie ahead of them, they proceeded forward.

Megan knew in her heart that living with a man when she was not married to him was not the Christian thing to do. Her stomach even felt unsettled about the decision she was making. From her perspective, though, there was no other alternative.

She wasn't going to stay in his family's house to be emotionally abused anymore, and she knew she couldn't go home. Since her heart didn't understand the spiritual damage it would do to live with him without being married, she didn't much care. She saw it as a way of making sure they were right for each other. She had seen the destruction divorce had brought about. Megan justified the idea of living with Ken as a way to make sure they could be together and were compatible before saying "I do".

From quite a distance, Bethany ached for her daughter's soul. She didn't want her living in sin but it was clear there was no stopping her now.

Megan was going to do what she wanted to do, regardless of her mother's feelings. She wanted the freedom she believed this choice would bring.

Bethany felt she had to give in, so she signed consent for marriage, and their wedding plans began. Everything about this situation made Bethany's skin crawl. She felt as though her daughter was making the worst mistake of her life. To her dismay, she was not able to talk sense into her.

The sooner she could get married, the better Megan's soul would be. Bethany cut every corner she could when it came to the traditional wedding bliss. She wanted to get the ball rolling as fast as possible, for the sake of her daughter's soul.

Bethany's first desire was for her daughter to know God and have an eternity with Him. However, she did not feel that would be the case if she knowingly allowed them to live together while being unwed. She saw her choice in signing the consent as the lesser of two evils.

Bethany was not the only one unsure about the marriage. Megan's three sisters and her dad were constantly voicing their opinions regarding her unwise choice.

Although Ken was a nice enough guy, he did have moments when his temper made Megan question what she was doing. She went through with her plans, though, because those moments seemed minor to the freedom she felt. Living in her own place with no parent to tell her what to do was fun. And the flowers and candy he surprised her with on a regular basis were romantic.

Little did Bethany know, Megan was feeling a lot of sorrow from being in this relationship. He was not exactly what she had in mind when thinking of her future husband.

One miscarriage after another took place while living with Ken. She knew there were many reasons why things like this could happen to a woman. According to her family, though, it was because God would not bless her if she was not married.

They had no idea the force with which Ken laid upon her. He never actually struck her. He would throw things in the direction of her head, punch a hole in the wall, barely missing her face just to warn her, screamed horrific profanity at her, and violently bedded her on a daily basis.

She continued to put up with the "loving relationship" façade. She didn't want to have to admit that she had made yet another mistake in judgment. She didn't want to believe that no one could love her.

She foolishly thought he would change after they were married.

Maybe God would bless her with a great marriage, but she had to be married first. If what her family said was true, then he would have to change once they were married. Only then would she feel what real love was supposed to feel like.

It wasn't exactly the wedding she had hoped for. She did not wear the dress of her dreams. The reception was anything but a fancy occasion. But to her, none of that mattered if the abuse would stop. Megan also yearned for her parents to respect her again.

She had great hopes that would be the case now that God could bless their marriage.

To her surprise, the abuse continued. Why wasn't God working in their marriage? Didn't the Bible teach that two become one flesh and husbands are supposed to love their wives? Megan thought, bewildered at the idea that God forgot about her marriage.

Nothing had changed. In fact, it got worse, because now she had no way to escape. As often as possible, he was all too willing to clue her in on this fact.

Ken enlisted into the Armed Forces. Oddly enough, even though he would not be around to bully her, Megan felt sad and trapped. He was a nasty sort of man but a constant in her life.

The first few weeks without him were pleasant. She was able to come and go as she pleased. She could purchase things without asking his permission. She was able to sleep in and stay up, no longer was she under constant supervision.

He was sent to the other side of the country, in preparation for his help in the Gulf War that neither of them understood.

She wrote him almost daily, even though he was the way he was. It was as if she was keeping a diary. Megan wanted to inform him of everything, because she did care for his safety and part of her did love him. It was the one way she felt less lonely as she was back to being friendless.

She long ago lost all the friends she had in high school. Once they moved in together, he made sure to not let her out of his sight. Since none of her old friends cared enough to reignite their relationship, she made new ones by going out to clubs while he was gone.

ROOTED WISDOM:

• What does Scripture say about premarital sex?

• Do you believe your purity can be destroyed or restored?

• Read Jeremiah 30:17 | Joel 2:25-26 | Isaiah 1:18 | 2 Corinthians 5:17. What does the Bible say about restoration?

- Were there any bad choices you saw Megan making or do you think she was justified with her behavior?

- What are your thoughts about God blessing marriages and not blessing people who live together out of wedlock? Try to defend your view with Scripture.

- How do you think Bethany and Joshua could have supported their daughter?

- Would her parents have a deeper influence on her if they would have handled the situation differently? Describe how you believe they should have handled it.

- How would the church be a support to this family at this time?

CHAPTER SEVEN: COMFORTLESS

"I will not leave you comfortless: I will come to you."
~ John 14:18, KJV

Though she was not nearly old enough to drink, that didn't stop her. She managed to lose herself in several heavily mixed drinks that men bought for her while out partying. It was her escape from sorrow.

She did not believe she had anyone to lean on. Sadly, she eventually even gave up on figuring out where God was.

Megan stopped caring what others would think of her. She ultimately just gave in and began living the life people believed she was living. She had a couple of casual affairs while Ken was gone at basic training. It was something to do to pass the time and make her feel wanted. She would not allow herself to become emotionally involved with any of them. In her mind, emotional involvement meant devastation. She was done with men using her heart and trampling all over it.

This time she was determined to be the user.

Ken returned to many warnings from his family and friends. His wife had blatantly been unfaithful. If he believed it, he did not make his awareness known.

Megan suspected it was because he was just as unfaithful, according to the rumors his closest friends spread.

Without any discussion or even a heads up, he moved her halfway across the country. He would be stationed there for the next year or so. Miles away from anything familiar, he achieved his goal of keeping her under lock and key.

Megan loved the beauty of her new hometown with its stately pine trees and luscious green grass. Everything smelled so crisp and fresh but she could only enjoy it by taking walks with his permission.

Ken would not allow her to go to the store without him, meet new people, or even go to church.

Megan longed for church, not because she felt she needed God. Why would she need Him when He never seemed to notice her? No, church was a place she knew from childhood where people would befriend her.

She had no plans of telling people how he treated her. She just wanted to feel like a normal person in society. She never even dared to share her feelings or reality with her family. If Ken was home while she was on the phone, he would listen in.

A few times, while living there, family members would come visit them. From the outside, everything looked picturesque. On the inside, she wanted to scream out for help. The only thing that stopped her from doing so was the potential of hearing the "I told you so" or the possibility of him finally changing for the better.

Once people were not around, things went back to the usual. It was easy enough to keep her away from everything and everyone. Ken had the only car they owned with him at all times.

A year went by, and at the age of eighteen, in the spring of 1996, she was free again. He was deployed overseas so she packed her bags and flew home to her mama.

Joshua and Bethany bought her a plane ticket as a gift so that she could come for a visit. They felt she needed cheering up, believing she missed Ken and was lonely there without any friends.

Her return flight was open ended so she could stay as long as she liked. With Ken gone, there was no need to rush back. Despite the fact that she still did not share her real life with her family, it still was nice to be home being waited on.

He wasn't happy with what she pulled, but Ken wrote her regularly. At first his letters were filled with rage and threats, demanding she move back to their home. After a while, they became soft and heartfelt, begging her to return and how much he missed her.

She had been gone for more than six months and had yet to reserve a return flight.

When he finally returned from war, Ken pleaded with her to come back, promising to change. He had seen brutality, and he wanted nothing of it.

She gave in because he sounded quite convincing in his sincerity.

At first, everything seemed sweet. The military even moved them closer to where their parents lived. It made her feel good to know she was closer to her parents, if they were needed.

The sweet quickly became the sour.

They lived on the base but still with only one vehicle, so she was only able to walk the neighborhood.

Megan did manage to meet a few other military wives, but their friendship was only superficial. Because of how possessive and suspicious Ken was, she didn't dare share with the ladies what was going on in her house. Who knew how long it would be before they told their husbands? And her words would eventually make their way back to Ken.

She couldn't help but think that maybe their husbands were as controlling as hers.

If she took a walk, she needed to inform him of what route she would be taking and how long she would be gone. There were two times that it took her longer to get home than she had anticipated. He came looking for her, guiding her tightly by her forearm home.

She wasn't purposefully late on those occasions; she just happened to get detoured because of construction on the base. That did not matter to Ken. Whenever this occurred, she was not permitted to take walks for a few weeks. Once again, she was feeling trapped in her own house.

Megan desperately wanted to run. How could she run without money or any form of transportation? How could she make it? These thoughts were so consuming that she couldn't help but dream of ways to break free from him.

One afternoon, she anonymously inquired about divorce for a "friend" through the law office on base. Megan was basically told that the military would protect the enlisted over the civilian any day and for any reason.

She felt so defeated but then the unthinkable happened.

The test was positive. The test was positive. The test was positive.

Could this really be happening? Megan wondered while holding the stick in her hand with tears in her eyes. She couldn't decide if this was good news or bad news.

She yearned to be a mother after having had so many miscarriages already and felt as though this might be the one time someone would love her unconditionally. It did bring about the fear of another miscarriage. And an even greater fear of being forever tied to a man who meant only harm to her was daunting.

Would he finally change now that she was giving him a child? Her mind wondered to a blissfully happy version of her life. She couldn't help but question what this baby would bring.

The more and more pregnant she became, the less violence he displayed. He still maintained his obsessively watchful eye on every move she made.

Megan often felt like she was being stalked. The friends she had made would approach her with questions of why her husband was calling their house checking up on her. She just played it off as though he wanted to make sure she was okay, since she was very pregnant.

Late summer, Lily was born. With no family around and friends who were nervous to be near Ken, Megan felt extremely isolated.

She had heard of women suffering from post-partum depression but wasn't sure if what she was experiencing was the same. She took care of Lily like a mother should but cried most of the day.

Ken managed to be the perfect absentee father. He was either gone to work or gone supportively while at home. He still persistently spouted out negativity and colorful names at her. He refused to assist in any care and keeping of their little girl.

Her body ached, not just from the birth of Lily but also from running on very little sleep.

Lily needed to be fed and changed round the clock. Unfortunately she was the only one willing to take on that task. Her emotions got the better of her, and it felt as though she cried more than she breathed. Megan cried while in bed, eating, taking care of Lily, using the bathroom, and even showering.

Ken soon became bored with Megan and hung out more with his work buddies. Despite his own expeditions, he was still not willing to let up on keeping her locked up.

Ken would come home at all hours of the night. Megan began to sleep in the spare bed in Lily's room. Everything about him irritated her. She segregated herself from him, especially from the marriage bed. Her irritation did not begin when her depression set in. It only increased.

Megan knew Ken had begun masturbating while she was pregnant. His sexual drive was too much for her, physically and emotionally. She was grossed out by his overwhelming demand of sex. Megan outright denied him as often as she could get away with it. The more he pleasured himself, the sicker she was with him.

She tried to confront him several times but he just lied. She would wake up in the middle of the night from a noise or because she had to use the restroom.

She would catch him engrossed in himself over the toilet, in the shower, or in his bed. On every single occasion he had a great excuse. "Scratching, using the restroom, washing, but certainly not that" were always his replies.

After Lily was born and she was staying in a different room, he became a little lazier about hiding his extracurricular activity.

At the wee hours of the morning, before the sun even rose, on a military PT day, Megan woke up to a noise. She quietly walked down the hall, noticed the light in the bathroom was on, and the shower was running.

He must be back from PT, she thought to herself. As she slowly opened the door, hoping to use the bathroom, she could see through the clear plastic shower curtain that he was at it again. Water was cascading down his back. His face was turned towards the nozzle with his eyes closed as he obsessively stroked. He was on the verge of finishing, "Caught you red handed, you liar!"

At the sound of Megan's voice Ken startled into the present with an awkward laugh. He sheepishly stated, "I really wanted you, but you were sleeping and I didn't want to wake you. This has never happened before."

With that lie, she knew it was over. She was exhausted from being married to a person who was a selfish lover, horrible friend, and an emotionally abusive liar.

ROOTED WISDOM:

- Have you ever experienced depression? If so, do you know what the root cause was and how have you maintained or healed from it?

- Read Galatians 5:16 | I Thessalonians 4:3-5 | James 1:14-15 | I Peter 2:11. What do the Scriptures say about masturbation?

- Read Proverbs 12:22 | Proverbs 13:5 |Proverbs 14:5 | Ephesians 4:29. What do the Scriptures say about lying?

- What services could the church provide for this couple?

- How could her family have supported her and her marriage to Ken?

- Do you think addiction became a wedge between them or was it just an excuse?

CHAPTER EIGHT: COMMAND

*"Have I not commanded you? Be strong and courageous.
Do not be frightened, and do not be dismayed, for the Lord
your God is with you wherever you go."
~Joshua 1:9*

"Daddy, will you come get us?" Joshua was surprised at the phone call. Seeing as how it was only five in the morning his time and she had never called to talk to him, only her mother, it caught him off guard.

"What's the matter? What is happening? Are you okay? Is someone hurt? Has Ken hurt you or Lily?" Joshua rambled on as though Megan wasn't even there.

"I'm fine, Dad, just tired," Megan said with a sorrowful tone.

"Why do you need me to come and get you then?" Confusion was surrounding Joshua as he tried waking a bit more for their conversation.

"I will not allow you to leave this house with my child!" Ken used an extremely life threatening force when he whispered this into her other ear while she was on the phone with her father. He made it crystal clear that he would use any means necessary to keep them both with him.

"I don't, Daddy, everything is fine." She was defeated but desperately wanted to be rescued by her hero.

"Are you sure because I can be there at the end of the day with a U-Haul and take you two out of there. I knew something was wrong. I knew he was a loser. You never should have married him." Joshua's irritation was increasing with each minute that passed.

"No. No, Dad. We're totally fine. I'm just bored. I will talk to you later. Love you, bye." She hung up the phone without waiting for a reply. Clearly there was no use in continuing the conversation.

Daddy couldn't save her this time. She wasn't altogether sure why he would want to; it was her choice to marry this "loser" as he put it.

Their routine went on as usual. She slept in a different room while he fondled himself whenever and wherever he wanted to.

Ken's emotionally destructive behavior carried over into his work, which is not okay by any means to the military. He refused to show up for PT, did not complete any of his duty roster assignments, and was disrespectful to officers and refused to solute them.

Ken was reprimanded a handful of times for mouthing off to his commanding officer and was believed to be to be bucking for a section eight discharge. He displayed fits of depression and admitted to suicidal thoughts. Instead, he was dishonorably discharged and encouraged to seek counseling.

They moved back to their hometown where their families lived.

They moved into a two bedroom apartment. She landed a great job at a local high school as an assistant teacher.

He went back to his high school job of auto specialist for Checker Auto Parts but did not take the advice given to him about counseling.

Megan had lost all respect for him. Being back in the public eye, she was able to make friends, female and male.

Reverting back to her old days, she once again started sleeping around. To mask her pain of being married to this jerk of a man and the fact that she was "that girl" again, she drank as well.

Megan wasn't a beer or wine drinker. She loved hard liquor mixed drinks. They were her numbing agent of preference. She would leave the house at night when Ken came home from work and not return until the bars were closed. There were several times she chose not to come home at all.

She believed her actions to be justified; after all, she wasn't the only parent Lily had. It was high time he put in his hours.

Typically sex was off the table, but Ken almost relished the idea of Megan's drinking. To him, it meant that she might come home wasted enough not to protest his advances and too wasted to fight off his force.

One such occasion proved to be particularly beneficial to him. A few weeks, later they discovered Megan was expecting another baby. In Ken's eyes, another baby meant less time for Megan to fool around. She would be sober for at least the next nine months. He saw it as just long enough to convince her to stay with him.

For some time now, he had been under the impression that she was contemplating leaving him. He thought she was possibly running away with one of her boyfriends, and he could not let that happen. Ken damaged anything he believed she would need in order to move out, hoping it would prevent her from doing so. The only things he left in one piece were the furniture, which they borrowed from his parents, and her clothes.

She was his and no one else's.

Although Megan no longer went out or slept around, she still found freedom working with the teenagers at the school.

Her ideals of having a baby who would love her unconditionally had diminished quite a bit now that Lily was two years old. Lily only had eyes for Daddy, a thought Megan could not wrap her head around. He basically only donated the sperm and hadn't done anything that should endear him to their daughter.

Now that she was pregnant again, maybe this time it would be different. She even tossed around the idea that Ken might be changing for the better finally. He was beginning to do sweet things for her like when they were dating in high school.

The pregnancy was an easy one, which gave Megan extra time to consider all of her options. She didn't feel as though God was with her. She didn't want to rely on her parents and she realized Ken was never truly going to change. He still displayed his abusive behaviors, spat out nasty remarks, and stalked her. How would a new baby change that?

After the first of the year, Hope was born. Lying in the hospital bed looking down on her sleeping babe, she made a silent vow. She did not want to allow her or her girls to continue to live under his roof in that hate-filled house.

It took weeks to recover and feel up to full speed. Megan started doing her research. She had never been a single mom and had heard how difficult it was. She went apartment hunting.

Every day after work, she would take a new route home to stop in to see a floor plan. She collected all the information she could get about the residence. She kept a journal and folder at work with all the information she collected. She had a packet which included a divorce attorney's contact information, a budget, a private savings account, contact numbers of friends, and any other tidbit she believed to be relevant.

Ken knew nothing of her plans.

One early spring morning while Ken was at work, Megan moved out. She only managed to move into an apartment across the street. It was all hers, and he had no access to it.

Four of her friends arrived with a truck, helped her pack all of her belongings, which wasn't much, and moved her life five hundred feet away. The move did not require four additional people or even

NOT JUST SOMEBODY'S DAUGHTER

a truck for that matter, but it was nice to have the company. The apartment was perfect for her.

As she gathered the last box on the kitchen counter, she replaced it with divorce papers. She left the key next to it, locked the door behind her, and walked out.

Something so freeing came over her. She was courageous for the first time in her entire life. It was the real heroic as-seen-in-the-movies courage.

She was bursting with excitement at the possibilities she now had available and within her reach. There would be no more worrying about how Ken will react. She did not care what his reaction would be. She no longer worried about him finding out whatever she had done or said without his permission. She would no longer be making excuses for him to her friends or wondering if he was watching her from a distance. She was free.

If only for the briefest of moments, she was happy.

Ken, of course, protested at some length. He begged her to come home. He threatened to have the kids taken away from her. He told her to watch her back. The police were called a couple of times when he tried attacking her at work. They let him off each time with a warning of what would happen if he continued his pursuit.

She could tell he was blown away that she managed to actually leave him.

A few weeks went by, and his rage got the better of him at their court hearing. The judge recommended he seek counseling and watch his tone. He warned Ken that his temper would make it very easy for him to award Megan with full custody so Ken backed off.

He hated her, everything about her, and wanted nothing to do with her. He signed the papers. Only a few short months later, the divorce was finally complete. Aside from having to exchange the girls every week, they lived their separate lives.

Most of Megan's friends said she was crazy. Her parents were furious because God hates divorce, but then Megan never really did what others told her to do. Why should their opinions matter to her, because they didn't really know Ken the way she had anyhow? Only one friend from work stood by her, Adam, and he intimidated the snot out of Ken.

ROOTED WISDOM:

- Describe a time in your life when you felt as though you needed to be rescued.

- What suggestions would you have for Megan about her marriage to Ken?

- Was Megan justified in forcing Ken to participate in parenting Lily? Try to defend your answer with Scripture.

- Describe a time when you dared to do something out of protection for yourself and your loved ones, knowing it might be dangerous.

- Megan's family told her "God hates divorce" but how do you think He would feel about what occurred in her marriage to Ken? Try to defend your response with Scripture.

- How could Megan's parents have been a support to her?

- How could the church be a support to Megan?

CHAPTER NINE: CONFRONTATION

"Be on your guard! If your brother sins, rebuke him;
and if he repents, forgive him."
~Luke 17:3

Megan had met Adam at work one morning when she was still pregnant with Hope. He was a student at a nearby college and was part of a work/study program that volunteered hours tutoring Math. He was a bit odd and awkward around women. There was no doubt that he was a total nerd, in a good way. He was so smart.

She discovered right away how smart he was when she overheard him explaining Calculus to one of her students. He was the graceful image of an Olympic gymnast teaching a Summersault with effortless precision.

He was dressed in blue jeans with a belt, a polo shirt tucked in, thick wire-rimmed glasses, and a tightly faded haircut. He was every bit a mom's dream of a man for her daughter but certainly not her type.

She loved the dangerous, scary-looking sort that parents have nightmares about and cry over with worry.

She brushed him off as a friend and thought nothing of his sexy smile, at least for a while. She did not need his biceps distracting her, nor did she want his protruding pectoral muscles causing her to lose focus on what to do with her life.

They talked as chums and nothing more.

He told her about growing up in a small town. They laughed about him having a roommate that snored a lot. He even talked a lot about nerdy things she didn't really understand.

In turn, she confided in him about how afraid she was of her husband. She confessed to wanting to leave so many times but not finding the strength needed to get the job done. She admitted to how unprepared she was for being a single mom.

"You are a stronger person than you know, Megan. Decide what you want to do and just do it. Don't let fear stand in the way of being the person you are supposed to be," Adam offered with a pleasant smile.

He had faith in her when no one else seemed to possess it.

Months after the divorce was final, that following spring, they started dating. They had gone to the movies several times, just as friends, as a way to get away from work and life. It was a peaceful and safe way of tuning out the world. Their first official date wasn't really a date at all.

One afternoon when both of them were done with work, she drove to his apartment to have dinner. They just got take out from Jack-in-the-Box but had the most amazing time learning about each other.

They stayed up talking all night long. Sharing the most secretive details of their lives was wonderful. Everything, from where they grew up to the hurts they felt, was on the table for discussion.

He knew everything about her, except for intimacy.

Megan began to really notice how attractive he was. He had the most captivatingly shaded brown eyes that seemed to dance as she talked. His eyelashes were so long they mesmerized her.

Adam Knight looked like what she imagined an Adonis would look like. He had a perfectly toned body with muscles that desired to rescue a damsel in distress. His skin complexion could be considered a close resemblance to smooth and silky caramel. She had never known a smile that had the ability to cause her on several occasions to lose her train of thought. But his did.

They hit it off immediately.

Their dating rituals were not exactly what one would call ideal. Since he was a college student without a car who lived twenty minutes away and she a single mom with two kids to look after, it was difficult. Her bank account usually only had pennies in it, but they made every effort to make things work.

They saw each other at work for the rest of the school year. Occasionally, they would get together on the weekends when he didn't have to study. It just looked to be too hard to care for one another as their lives were painstakingly separate. Needless to say, they did not spend as much time as they would have liked to together.

She would have liked to have spent what little money she had pursuing him, but her girls needed to come first. She loved them deeply and wanted to be good at being a mom, but it didn't come easy.

Megan still had bouts of depression that reared its ugly head often. The more she let the sadness in, the harder it was to parent. Her girls were spoiled at their dad's house and even more so when they spent time with his parents. When they would return to her, all they could say was she wasn't doing anything right and that their dad loved them more. She was manipulated into believing that nothing she was doing for them was good enough.

Megan contemplated giving Ken full custody. Lily and Hope acted as though they wanted nothing to do with her, so why not free herself from the bondage that smothered her opportunities? Having children was no walk in the park. It was a full-time, ungratifying job. They required more from her than she knew how to give, and she was exhausted.

Megan would get up at four-thirty in the morning to get ready for work, which took an hour. Then spend the next hour making breakfast and getting the girls ready for daycare. She drove thirty minutes to drop them off for the day and then another thirty minutes to get to work. She worked from seven-thirty in the morning until four-thirty in the afternoon. After picking up the girls, they would make it home by five-thirty just in time to start dinner. Once dinner was done, Megan would spend close to an hour playing with them until it was time for bath and bed. This routine went on daily when they were in her care.

When summer break began, she decided to change jobs. She spent way too much money on child care. It was her hope this new job would change that. She was able to be home during the weekdays and work her forty hours over the weekend when Ken had their daughters.

Megan began working at a group home for troubled teens and loved it. It was her dream job but brought about a decent pay cut. She didn't believe it would cause too many problems since she no longer had to pay for childcare. Even though the pay wasn't that great, she was able to spend more time with her girls. She had also hoped that it would give Adam and her more uninterrupted time, but that was far from possible.

He was becoming busier and busier with school. When he wasn't at school, he was off drinking with friends. He did like Megan and her girls, but he wasn't sure if he was ready for an instant, full-time family.

Although they enjoyed each other, they were not really that serious. She hoped they would be, but he was not ready to admit his feelings for her or how important she was to him.

Since it did not look as though they would be tied together anytime soon, she knew she could not rely on him. It wasn't long before the bills began to pile up, and her job was just not covering them well enough. Megan was never in charge of the budget while married to Ken, so she was unaware of how to manage money. Although she did not have to pay for childcare, the rent, the electric, and the water bill was still due each month. Now that the girls were with her all week long, on only one income, groceries went out faster than they came into her fridge.

Her purse strings were becoming tighter and tighter, so she dared to do something that made every ounce of her body sick. She became an exotic dancer at a private club, two afternoons a week. She knew this job would upset a lot of people. But being a single mom was more expensive than she had anticipated, and the only two people whose opinions really mattered to her at this point were her daughters. She was willing to do the unthinkable.

Megan walked into the club and filled out a liability paper. She had to audition for the audience and the club owner. She got offered the job on the spot and was told to start that same day. She had to provide her own costumes, make-up, and whatever accessories she needed so she went shopping.

She had never really owned trashy undergarments. It took her some time to pick out ones she felt comfortable in. Within a day, the credit card she charged the items on was paid off. Each day she worked, she had money left over to burn. Her bills were paid in full. Her fridge was stocked. Her gas tank was full. She was even able to take her girls out for special things, not to mention go on a few nice dates with Adam.

Life seemed great, and she felt stress free again.

Her head was telling her wonderful positive things, but her stomach would turn just a bit each day she drove to the club. Worse than that, though, was the ache in her heart when she thought about her daughters finding out what she did to pay the bills.

Megan had never been a good liar, and her redemption came in the form of her older sisters, Valerie and Cassidy. She hadn't seen either of them on a regular basis, just during the holidays, and even then Valerie kept to herself. Megan brought Lily and Hope to Cassidy's for a birthday party, toting extravagant gifts. She probably should have downplayed the presents, but Megan deliberately wanted to be noticed.

"How are you making all this money?" Cassidy questioned.

"I have been dancing for the strip club. It's no big deal. I just need to support my girls," Megan pointedly stated.

Valerie, overhearing the conversation and with her ultra-intimidating mama bear voice, warned, "If you don't quit right now, I will tell Mom what you have been up to!"

Her sisters gave one another an approval glance then glared daggers into Megan's eyes. It felt as though she was having a staring contest with professional poker players.

They held all the cards and were serious about playing them. Although she had done many horrible things in her past, this could be considered the worst. Most of her past was well known by all, even her mother who was continuously disappointed. Nothing would have come close in comparison to this where her mother was concerned.

With one quick statement, the duo was able to create an unprecedented shame eating away at Megan's gut.

With that, she quit the next day, relieved to be rid of it, and didn't return.

The nice dates and special things for her girls stopped as well. She did manage to put money into savings, so she was able to continue working at the group home without worrying about her bills.

A couple of months later, Megan was offered the manager position at one of the homes. It gave her a significant increase in pay, which came just in the nick of time, because her savings account was nearing the bottom of the barrel.

Adam also began to make more of an effort in building their relationship. He started asking her to join him and his friends on outings, like hiking. He even made her dinner and wanted her to meet his family.

They were alone far too often by their own choice. One afternoon, they became intimate.

She knew this wasn't his first time but was completely ashamed at who she had been. She worried he would think less of her if he knew all the gory details.

They were both raised in Christian homes and tried to stand by everything they were taught, minus sex, of course. The sex was great with Adam, but she wasn't sure how long it would last. He still was not fully committed to their relationship, and she didn't know why. They had been dating for two years now. What was holding him up?

Instead of waiting around to discover the answer, she decided to tell him the whole truth about her sexual encounters. She sat him down and explained she had something she needed to share with him.

Adam listened intently. He didn't even look surprised, and she couldn't tell if that was a good sign or bad. She told him about her dancing and all the abuse she endured. She left absolutely nothing out.

He reassured her things were fine and nothing had changed, but she could tell something had.

Their time together became shorter and shorter. He stopped inviting her places. He stopped calling her on a regular basis. It seemed easy for him to just let her go.

Megan's heart ached. She finally felt love again, so why was it so difficult? She went over to his apartment to confront him about why he was avoiding her.

A friend and classmate of his, Greg, was there. She wanted to speak with him alone but Greg didn't get the hint.

"What is going on with you? Why have you been avoiding me? Why are you putting your friends ahead of me?" She demanded with tears in her eyes.

"Megan, now is not the time. Let me walk you to your car." Adam walked her downstairs as Greg followed.

When she reached her car, she turned towards him with longing in her eyes. "Why won't you just answer my questions?"

"Adam you don't need this witch. There are plenty more girls with less baggage than her. You can get laid anytime. You don't need her," Greg declared without even looking in Megan's direction.

With complete embarrassment overshadowing his face, Adam spoke up. "School comes first, even before you. I don't have time for this mess. You are making things too difficult."

He looked hurt but certainly did not say anything about it.

Rage filled Megan's face. Sobs came pouring out as Megan began shouting profanity, while pointing her finger in Greg's face. Turning towards Adam, she continued, "And you can go take a flying leap!" She got in her car, slammed the door, and sped away. She was done.

ROOTED WISDOM:

- Do you believe relationships that last are supposed to be easy or hard, and why?

- Do you think Megan should have given custody of the girls to Ken?

- What do you think was holding Adam back from committing to Megan?

- Do you feel Megan compromised her morals for her daughters' welfare? Would you have done the same?

- What motives do you think Valerie had behind her threat to tell their mother about what Megan was doing?

- How do you think Megan handled the confrontation with Adam?

- What social services do you think Megan should have been involved in?

- What services could the church provide for her? Their relationship? Her parenting?

CHAPTER TEN: CROWNED

*"You shall be a crown of beauty in the hand of the LORD,
and a royal diadem in the hand of your God."*
~Isaiah 62:3, ESV

For the next three hours, her phone would not stop ringing. The first time she heard it ring was shortly after she returned home from Adam's apartment.

Since she believed they had just ended it, it never would have occurred to her that he would be on the other end of the receiver.

She answered, "Hello?"

"Hi, Megan." Adam said softly.

She hung up quickly and with such power she thought she might have broken the receiver.

The phone just kept ringing. For three hours it rang and rang. She knew it was him but could not bring herself to pick up the phone. All that was on the other end of that line was more pain.

She tried to go to sleep, hoping he would give up. He didn't want to be with her anyway, so he was bound to give up at some point. The phone just kept ringing.

At one o'clock in the morning, she finally answered. "What do you want?"

"Please talk to me." His voice was audibly in pain. It was evident he had been crying.

"Talk," Megan demanded.

"Will you please come over here and talk to me? I want to speak to you in person, not over the phone. Please?" Adam begged.

"Fine. I will be there in a bit." She hung up the phone and grabbed her keys.

Why was she giving him another chance? All he was going to do was use her and toss her aside again. Why did she continue to fall for one creep after another? The thoughts raced through her mind as she drove as slowly as possible back to his apartment. With each stop light, she considered turning around.

Megan had been told most of her life that God had a plan for her. She was told God had the perfect man for her and in time He would provide him to her. She had thought Adam was the one when they first started dating because he was unlike any other man she had been with. He loved on her girls and treated them as his own.

Could she have been wrong about him this whole time? She turned the car around to head home just before turning onto his street. Her brain kept telling her Enough is enough. Just cut all ties and move on. It's not like he is going to come looking for you. He doesn't have a car. You could change your phone number and then that would be that.

She drove for two more miles, having thought she made the right decision when all of a sudden her heart spoke up. Turn this car around and hear him out. Who said love was supposed to be easy? Give him a chance. Everyone makes mistakes. He clearly knows he did or why else would he have spent three hours annoying you with phone calls?

Megan's car screeched as she did a quick one-eighty.

She slowly opened his door and was greeted with open arms. He embraced her tightly, not wanting to let her go as her arms hung lifelessly at her side.

"I'm so sorry. Please don't leave me. I don't want to lose you. I made a mistake. What can I do to make things better?" Adam cried as he spoke to her, looking deeply into her eyes.

"Why the change of heart, Adam? And why did you say those horrible things in the first place? You must believe them or why else would you say them?" Megan whispered, not willing to look him in the eyes because she knew they would melt her harshness away.

"My parents." He gulped the reason out of his system. "They have called daily to try to convince me to leave you. They don't want me to be with someone who has been with others, previously divorced, and already has kids. They want me to focus on school and my career before I settle down. They told me if I stay with you that they will not help with my bills or school anymore. They even asked Greg to try to talk me out of dating you. Between the two of them, I just got tired and gave up. I am so sorry. The stress had gotten to me, and I was too weak to fight anymore."

"So why the change?" She argued.

"You are my heart. I do not want to spend the rest of my life with them. I am an adult who can make my own decisions, and it is about time I start doing that. You are who I want. Their opinion does not matter so long as you are with me."

"Will you go to couple's counseling with me?" She questioned, assuming he would say no and she could leave. It would be her excuse for breaking it off for good.

"If that is what it takes, sure." He surrendered in defeat.

"I just think it is best. I have issues because of my past relationships. You have issues because of your ex-girlfriend and your parents. If you are willing to go with me, then we can work on getting back together. If we are going to be in a relationship, then let's do the work," Megan gently ordered in hopes they could grow together.

Counseling helped a lot. Megan was so sure of being with him that she proposed on his birthday.

With excitement, he said, "YES!"

The following spring, he asked her. She made it official by holding her hand out to his engagement ring. Adam asked Lily and Hope if he could marry their mom and told them he would love them forever. He said they would be a family, and the girls hugged his neck tight in reply.

They moved in together, and the date was set. They had been going to church as a couple for a while, but it wasn't until six weeks before the wedding that things began to change.

"Babe, if we are going to be married soon, I think we should do it the right way," Adam spoke up one evening just before bed.

Puzzled, Megan asked, "What do you mean?"

"Well, we are both supposed to be Christians, and yet, we are having sex before marriage," he boldly stated.

"Yeah, so?" she questioned. "We have been doing that this whole time."

"So, I think we should abstain for the rest of our engagement. It will make our honeymoon night more special. Would you be okay with that?" His face looked as though he meant business. They had just experienced a wonderful sermon at church about how marriage is three threads woven together to make one strand. The minister explained that it is only made strong when God is intertwined from start to finish. Adam's heart was convicted when he heard him say that God will bless a marriage that honors His will. That was all it took for Adam to have the strength to make the godly decision to abstain. He wanted his marriage to his love to be blessed.

Megan's heart soared with the idea that this man wanted the two of them to be renewed in the eyes of God. She was so delighted that he wanted to make this pledge with her. She could somehow feel God talking to her. She wasn't sure how that was possible, but she knew it was Him.

Sex was a major weakness for Megan. She found Adam extremely irresistible and knew she would blow it. She feared she would let him down by either cheating on him or seducing him until he gave in.

A tiny whisper filled her heart, Trust in the Lord with all your heart and lean not on your own understanding. In all your ways acknowledge Him and He will direct your paths.

God was speaking to her!

He gave her strength and brought her back to Him every time she tried to take matters into her own hands, during the remainder of their engagement.

Six weeks later as Megan walked down the aisle, she suddenly understood that this was the second time she was going to take this vow. With Lily by Adam's side and Hope at hers, she wanted it to be different. She did not want to make the same mistakes in this marriage as she had in the past. It dawned on her that the only thing missing in her previous marriage was her relationship with God.

During the service, the pastor asked everyone for silence. He began to pray for a united family that would serve the Lord. All four of them held hands and bowed their heads as the pastor prayed out loud. Then he told Adam, Megan, and their girls to pray silently together. While holding onto Lily and Hope, Adam prayed for their new family and the future they would have. Megan worshipped the Lord to herself.

She thanked God for never giving up on her. She thanked Him for keeping her alive when she did dangerous things. She thanked Him for bringing Adam into her life. She thanked Him for loving her deeply and forgiving her for all of her mistakes. She thanked Him for His Son who came to save even her.

Then she asked for Him to continue to walk beside her.

"Lord, please help me to be the godly wife You have designed me to be. Help me to be the godly mother You have blessed me to be. Help me to be the godly friend You need me to be to those who do not know You. I want to live my life for You alone. I cannot be this person without you. I cannot do any of this alone. You are my Savior, my Rock, and my Redeemer! Stand by my side and direct my paths. I may still have a hard time and still make bad choices, but whatever You need to do to get my attention, do it. One day I will make You proud, Father. Please forgive my past and help me with the future. In Your Son's name, I humbly pray, AMEN."

She had taken a moment to ask His forgiveness and renewed her faith in Him. It felt as though she was being supernaturally hugged, and she was given a vision of angels rejoicing.

With the words, "I do," their life began. Two became one flesh. As they walked down the aisle, people reached out to hug them. Joshua wrapped his arms around Megan, leaned in towards her ear, and whispered, "Sweetheart, you are the most beautiful bride. I love you with all my heart. I am so proud of the lady you have become. You will always be my baby." He kissed her cheek as tears ran down to meet his lips. Her face flushed and her heart swelled at the reconciliation she believed God had just given to her.

As Megan continued to think about her kids and how they would grow up, she stroked Adam's hair. She thought about all the fun they had had. She thought about the sorrows they had overcome. She thought about the moments of distance they had experienced in their marriage when times were tough.

As her mind unfolded a detailed map of their life together, she looked at his face in admiration. He loved her, despite her past. He accepted her as his gift from God. A smile rose across her face as she realized he was her gift.

An even bigger smile made her skin ache when it dawned on her that He blessed her with two amazing men to care for her. Megan was cherished by the father she turned out to be like, stubborn but loving, and the husband who protected the purity God saw in her.

God loved her, washing away the sins of her past. To Him, she was a priceless gem in His crown. She was not just somebody's daughter. She was His child. Megan was the daughter of the King of kings and Lord of lords!

ROOTED WISDOM:

- Do you listen to your head or heart more often? Which do you believe is usually correct?

- In Exodus 20:12, the Bible says that we are to "honor our father and mother". Do you think Adam made the right choice in sticking up for Megan against his parents?

- Do you believe Adam was sincere with his intentions to wait until marriage?

- In waiting those six weeks, do you believe based from verses that were read in previous chapters that Megan and Adam were made pure again? Why or why not?

- Why do you think Megan finally heard the Lord speaking to her?

- Read Deuteronomy 31:6. Do you believe He had always been there for her? Do you believe He is always there for you?

- What things could Megan do differently to protect the sanctity of this marriage?

- How could Adam be a support and encouragement to Megan so that she no longer struggles with her sexual addiction?

- What things could her parents do differently to protect the sanctity of this marriage?

- How might the church provide support to Adam and Megan's marriage?

SALVATION MESSAGE

*"He has saved us and called us to a holy life—not because
of anything we have done but because of his own purpose
and grace. This grace was given us in
Christ Jesus before the beginning of time."
2 Timothy 1:9, NIV.*

The Bible teaches of the free gift of Salvation through Jesus Christ. In order to receive this gift of eternal life you must:

1. Admit you are a sinner.

*"All have sinned and fall short of the glory of God."
Romans 3:23, NIV*

*"If we confess our sins, He is faithful and righteous to
forgive us our sins and
to cleanse us from all unrighteousness."
I John 1:9, NASB*

2. Believe that Christ the Son of God died on the cross taking our deserved punishment on Himself, was buried, after three days rose from the grave, and is seated at the right hand of God. He will return for His followers soon. Be baptized as an external sign of your internal decision.

"He made Him who knew no sin to be sin on our behalf,
so that we might become the righteousness of God in Him."
2 Corinthians 5:21, NASB

"So Christ was sacrificed once to take away the sins of
many; and he will appear a second time, not to bear sin,
but to bring salvation to those who are waiting for him."
Hebrews 9:28, NIV

"But God demonstrates His own love toward us, in that
while we were yet sinners, Christ died for us."
Romans 5:8, NASB

"For if, while we were God's enemies, we were reconciled
to him through the death of his Son, how much more,
having been reconciled, shall we be saved through his life!"
Romans 5:10, NIV

"Whoever believes and is baptized will be saved, but
whoever does not believe will be condemned."
Mark 16:16, NIV

3. Commit your life to Christ by following His example.

*"For it is with your heart that you believe and are
justified, and it is with your mouth
that you profess your faith and are saved."*
Romans 10:10, NIV

*"For the grace of God has appeared that offers salvation to
all people. It teaches us to say 'No' to ungodliness and worldly
passions, and to live self-controlled, upright and godly lives
in this present age."*
Titus 2:11-12, NIV